CHILDREN
1990

A Report Card,
Briefing Book, and
Action Primer

CHILDREN'S DEFENSE FUND

Contents

Part I: Introduction

SOS AMERICA!
A MOMENT OF GREAT NATIONAL
OPPORTUNITY AND DANGER

SOS America!

A MOMENT OF GREAT NATIONAL OPPORTUNITY AND DANGER

The year 1989 was one of transforming events outside America—in Poland, the Soviet Union, China, Hungary, Czechoslovakia, East Germany, Romania, and all of Europe. As in 1848 or 1914, these irreversible changes and political tidal waves will have a profound effect on the lives of our children and grandchildren.

The year 1990 must be one of transforming action inside America. As we begin this last decade of the twentieth century, we must get to work rebuilding the moral and social foundations of our society, starting with our treatment of children. We must make it un-American for any child to grow up poor or without adequate child care, health care, food, shelter, education, and safety from neglect, abuse, and violence.

We have no moral or practical choice. The mounting crisis of our children and families is a rebuke to everything America professes to be. It also will bring America to its economic knees and increase violence and discord within this country unless we confront it. The number of children—soon to be young adults—in our society is dwindling. In the year 2000 there will be 4.1 million fewer Americans between the ages of 18 and 24 than there were in the mid-1980s. Increased competition abroad means that every one of them must be fully productive. Yet:

- Every eight seconds of the school day, an American child drops out (552,000 during the 1987-1988 school year).
- Every 26 seconds of each day, an American child runs away from home (1.2 million a year).
- Every 47 seconds, an American child is abused or neglected (675,000 a year).
- Every 67 seconds, an American teenager has a baby (472,623 in 1987).
- Every seven minutes, an American child is arrested for a drug offense (76,986 a year).
- Every 30 minutes, an American child is arrested for drunken driving (17,674 a year).
- Every 36 minutes, an American child is killed or injured by guns (14,6000 a year).
- Every 53 minutes, an American child dies because of poverty (10,000 a year).

3

One Day in the Lives of American Children

17,051	women get pregnant.
2,795	of them are teenagers.
1,106	teenagers have abortions.
372	teenagers miscarry.
1,295	teenagers give birth.
689	babies are born to women who have had inadequate prenatal care.
719	babies are born at low birthweight (less than 5 pounds, 8 ounces)
129	babies are born at very low birthweight (less than 3 pounds, 5 ounces)
67	babies die before one month of life.
105	babies die before their first birthday.
27	children die from poverty.
10	children die from guns.
30	children are wounded by guns.
6	teenagers commit suicide.
135,000	children bring a gun to school.
7,742	teens become sexually active.
623	teenagers get syphilis or gonorrhea.
211	children are arrested for drug abuse.
437	children are arrested for drinking or drunken driving.
1,512	teenagers drop out of school.
1,849	children are abused or neglected.
3,288	children run away from home.
1,629	children are in adult jails.
2,556	children are born out of wedlock.
2,989	see their parents divorced.
34,285	people lose jobs.

- Every school day, 135,000 American children bring guns to school. A child is safer in Northern Ireland than on the streets of America.
- Every day, 100,000 American children are homeless.

The statistics are even worse for poor and minority children. Yet these youngsters make up an increasingly large portion of the youth population—and, consequently, of our future work force.

Only two of 10 new work force entrants in the 1990s will be white males born in the United States. If we are to compete effectively in the world economy, we need minority and poor youngsters to produce, rather than become dependent on us or shoot at us. Those who do not want to invest in black or brown or poor children must remember this.

But all Americans need to confront the plain truth: Youngsters from every economic and racial group are neglected, adrift, and in trouble. And their troubles pose a greater threat to American security, prosperity, and ideals than any external enemy.

Who Do We Want To Be?

For nearly one-fourth of its life, our nation has focused much of its energy, ideology, and money on the Cold War—on establishing that we are "Not-Russia." Now that we must be something other than just "Not-Russia," we have an opportunity to build a future based on traditional American values of community, family, educational achievement, tolerance, and investment in the future.

What better time to begin than now, as we prepare for a new century? In 1990, 36 governorships, 6,257 other state offices, 34 Senate seats, and every seat in the U.S. House of Representatives are up for election. The officials who are elected will be making decisions critical to the child care, health, child welfare, education, and safety of children in every state and nationally. No other decisions are more important to the American future.

As citizens, we must tell candidates and elected officials that investing in children must come first rather than last on their list for concern and action. We must tell them that it is not military might that distinguishes us as Americans; it is our vision of liberty and justice for all: black, brown, yellow, red, and white, young and old, women and men. We must tell them that what will draw a world that is two-thirds nonwhite and poor to the American dream is our moral determination to be the best that we can be and to include all in the fruits of the earth. And we must tell them that what will heal our lost sense of community and national striving are our common hopes and dreams for our children.

The Nation's Report Card on Caring for Children: Unsatisfactory

America is not competitive with other industrialized nations in caring for its children and preparing for its future.

As the wealthiest nation on earth and the standard-bearer of Democracy, we have an "A" *capacity* to care for our children but an "F" *performance* on many key indicators of child well-being. By every measure, the U.S. performance is unsatisfactory.

- American one-year-olds have lower immunization rates against polio than one-year-olds in 14 other countries. Polio immunization rates for nonwhite babies in the United States rank behind 48 other countries, including Botswana, Sri Lanka, Albania, Colombia, and Jamaica.
- America's 1988 overall infant mortality rate lagged behind 18 other nations. In 1987 our nonwhite infant mortality rate ranked thirtieth compared with other countries' overall rates. A black child born in inner-city Boston has less chance of surviving the first year of life than a child born in Panama, North or South Korea, or Uruguay.
- In a study of eight industrialized nations (the United States, Switzerland, Sweden, Norway, West Germany, Canada, England, and Australia), America had the highest child poverty rate. Children are the poorest Americans.
- America has the highest teen pregnancy rates among six industrialized nations studied (including France, England and Wales, Canada, the Netherlands, and Sweden).
- America and South Africa are the only industrialized nations that fail to provide universal health coverage, child care, and parental leave for their children and parents.
- American school children know less geography than school children in Iran, less math than school children in Japan, and less science than school children in Spain.
- America invests a smaller portion of its GNP (gross national product) in child health than 18 other industrialized countries. It invests a smaller proportion of its GNP in education than six other industrialized countries.

The States' Report Card: Unsatisfactory

This inadequate national performance is reflected in the inadequate performance of all 50 states and the District of Columbia. CDF measured 10 basic indicators of progress in improving children's well-being and 10 basic indicators of state investments in children. Despite efforts by a number of states in recent years to expand children's programs, not a single state earned a decent grade. The highest score for any state, which went to Vermont, was only 65 out of 100 possible points.

- Only six out of the 50 states (Vermont, Maine, Massachusetts, Minnesota, Connecticut, and Delaware) received a grade of 50 percent or more.
- Twenty states—nearly half—received grades of 25 percent or less.
- The average state score was 32 percent—meaning that they received positive scores on only slightly more than six out of 20 indicators.

Progress in Improving Children's Well-Being

Some examples show how badly the states did on these 10 indicators of progress in improving the status of children:

- **Prenatal care:** Not a single state in the nation made the grade towards improved access to prenatal care at a rate that will meet the Surgeon General's 1990 goal of early prenatal care for 90 percent of all pregnant women.

6

States Grouped by Total Scores

Scores	States	Scores	States
10%	New Mexico	35%	Alabama
			Alaska
15%	Colorado		Michigan
	Idaho		North Dakota
	Kansas		Virginia
	South Dakota		
		40%	Illinois
20%	Arizona		Iowa
	Georgia		New Hampshire
	Kentucky		New Jersey
	Mississippi		New York
	Missouri		Pennsylvania
	Oklahoma		Rhode Island
			Washington
25%	District of Columbia		Wisconsin
	Indiana		
	Louisiana	45%	California
	Montana		Connecticut
	Nebraska		South Carolina
	North Carolina		
	Oregon	55%	Delaware
	Texas		Massachusetts
	Utah		Minnesota
	Wyoming		
		60%	Maine
30%	Arkansas		
	Florida	65%	Vermont
	Hawaii		
	Maryland		
	Nevada		
	Ohio		
	Tennessee		
	West Virginia		

- **Low birthweight:** Only five states have been making sufficient progress in reducing the proportion of infants born at low birthweight.
- **Child poverty:** In only two states—Delaware and New Hampshire—did childhood poverty fall even slightly between 1979 and 1985. Twelve states experienced child poverty increases of 50 percent or more.
- **Births to unmarried women:** Every state experienced an increase in the proportion of births that were to unmarried women; 29 had increases greater than the national average.

State Investment in Children

The states did just as badly when CDF measured their efforts on the 10 indicators of how much and how wisely they have invested in children. For example:

- **Medicaid coverage of pregnant women and infants:** Although prenatal care saves lives and dollars ($3 for every $1 invested), only 15 states at the end of 1989 were covering all pregnant women and infants with incomes below 185 percent of the federal poverty level, as permitted by federal law.
- **State supplementation of the Special Supplemental Food Program for Women, Infants, and Children (WIC):** Despite WIC's success in improving maternal and infant health and its cost effectiveness ($1 invested in WIC for pregnant women yields $3 in savings), only nine states and the District of Columbia supplemented their federal WIC allotment to provide food *and* nutrition services to additional women and children. Only 59 percent of all eligible women and children receive WIC benefits.
- **Quality child care:** Although parents place quality at the top of their child care concerns, only 30 states maintain child-to-caregiver staffing requirements for the care of infants in child care centers that meet the professionally accepted minimum safety standards.
- **Prevention of homelessness:** Both the supply and affordability of housing has decreased, leaving many families with children in unacceptable and expensive shelters and hotels on an emergency basis. Yet no state pays a monthly AFDC (Aid to Families with Dependent Children) benefit that ensures that typical inexpensive housing costs will be less than 30 percent of income, as HUD recommends. In 38 states, the cost of the lowest priced rental units exceeds the family's *entire* monthly AFDC payment.
- **Educational quality:** Smaller class size is an important step in increasing children's learning, but only seven states and the District of Columbia maintain class sizes that meet standards recommended by experts in the field.

What We Must Do To Place Children Higher on the Political Agenda

In 1988 both party platforms waxed eloquent about the importance of children to the national future. Presidential candidates and their spouses frequented child care centers and high schools as backdrops for their campaign stops. Many governors and members of Congress made eloquent speeches about the importance of children to the American future.

But in 1989 this rhetorical concern for children was too seldom evident in deed.

In Washington, the White House and Congress placed a higher priority on approving pay raises for themselves and spending $164 billion to bail out the savings and loan industry than on enacting a $1.75 billion comprehensive child care bill to provide safe, affordable, quality child care to the poorest 500,000 of the 10.5 million young children with mothers in the labor force. Although comparable child care bills passed both Houses of Congress after thorough debate and much compromise, $1.2 billion appropriated for child care in Fiscal Year 1990 and additional billions in tax credits to help low-income parents meet rising housing and food costs were lost because Congress could not find the time or the will to complete action. House Budget Committee Chair Leon Panetta said, "Child care was the sacrificial lamb."

In the states children did not fare any better. Increases in prison construction costs continued, while funding levels for such subsistence programs as Aid to Families with Dependent Children continued to erode. Many states failed to take advantage of massive federal funding, even when it was offered, to improve such important programs for children as Medicaid. Even though the federal government pays between 50 and 80 percent of the cost of providing Medicaid to all poor children younger than six, only 17 states chose to provide these benefits at the end of 1989. Moreover, many states have failed to invest their own funds in programs of proven effectiveness whose federal funding levels are inadequate. Despite the fact that Head Start is one of the most successful and cost-effective programs ever created for young children, 21 states fail either to supplement federal funding levels (which are adequate to reach only one in six eligible children) or to fund comparable state programs.

Speaking Out for Children

The challenge before us is to make clear to our political leaders that we are no longer willing to have children be sacrificial lambs or political pawns. Nor are we willing to accept rhetoric for action, cosmetic response for significant investment, or politically attractive responses that leave the underlying causes of child and family misery unaddressed.

It should not be so hard to get our political leaders to do what is right and sensible for children and the nation.

Our message of child and national crisis must be accompanied by a message of hope backed with specific solutions for change. We must let our political leaders know that some things do work; that early childhood investment is cheaper than ignorance, teen pregnancy, special education, and welfare dependency; that most poor children are not in an intractable underclass and do not require massive government intervention and resources. For most children at risk, a boost now and then or flexible help for the parents is enough. They need child care, not foster care; a check-up, not an intensive care bed; a tutor, not a guardian; a Head Start, not 12 years of special education; a scholarship, not an institutional placement. Their parents need higher wages, not public jobs. But it has been too hard to get them what they need—even when we know what to do and even when it saves us money in the long term.

We cannot go back and change the past decade's birth rates. But we can prevent and reduce our rising child, family, and human deficits. In the waning years of the twentieth century, doing what is right for children and doing what is necessary to save our national skins have converged.

In 10 years, when the new century dawns with new global economic and military challenges, America will be ready to compete economically and lead morally only if we:

- Stop cheating and neglecting our children for selfish, short-sighted, personal and political gain.
- Stop clinging to our racial past and recognize that America's ideals, future, and fate are as inextricably intertwined with the fate of its poor and nonwhite children as with its privileged and white ones.
- Love our children more than we fear each other and our perceived or real external enemies.
- Acquire the discipline to invest preventively and systematically in all of our children *now* in order to reap a better trained work force and more stable families *tomorrow*.
- Curb the desires of the overprivileged so that the survival needs of the less privileged may be met, and spend less on weapons of death and more on lifelines of constructive development for our citizens.
- Set clear national, state, city, community, and personal goals for child survival and development, and invest whatever leadership, commitment, time, money, and sustained effort are needed to achieve them.
- Get involved. Every parent, child care worker, educator, pediatrician, and citizen concerned about helping children should know what investments in children are needed and should attend town meetings; call, write, and visit your members of Congress, governor, mayor, and state legislators, and invite them to visit your congregation or organization.
- Begin to live our lives in less selfish and more purposeful ways, redefining success by national and individual character and service rather than by national consumption and the superficial barriers of race and class.

The cost of repairing our crumbling national foundation will be expensive in leadership, effort, time, and money. The cost of not repairing it, or patching it cosmetically, may be fatal.

Top Priorities for 1990

CDF's top 1990 priority—also shared by millions of American families—is the immediate enactment of a child care bill that is good for children and not just for politicians. There will be renewed attempts to pass a child care bill that would provide far less money ($200 million to $400 million total) than the $1.75 billion child care bill that passed both Houses in 1989 by healthy margins. Such a retreat would provide day care to hundreds of thousands fewer children. And despite increasing lip service to protecting children in day care, there will be attempts to eliminate basic health, safety, and quality protections for all children in day care. If the attempts succeed, and if politics rather than children are the bottom line of a child care bill, the child care crisis will grow. And the nation will pay.

10

Investments To Make and Savings To Gain

PROGRAM	SHORTFALL	PROGRAM BENEFIT FOR CHILDREN	COST SAVINGS
Special Supplemental Food Program for Women, Infants, and Children (WIC) provides nutritional help to the needy.	As of 1989, WIC served only 59 percent of those potentially eligible.	Reduces infant mortality and number of births at low birth-weight; improves nutritional outcomes for children in the first six years of life, including reduced anemia rates and better growth rates.	$1 invested in the pre-natal compo-nent of WIC saves as much as $3 in short-term hospital costs. Improved early nutrition has been shown to be effective in preventing retardation and consequent costs.
Medicaid, including Early and Periodic Screening, Diagnosis, and Treatment (EPSDT) services for children, puts health care within the reach of the uninsured poor.	As of 1987, less than half of America's poor pregnant women and children were covered by Medicaid.	Results in earlier prenatal care, increased birthweight, decreased neonatal and postneonatal mortality and morbidity, and fewer abnormalities among children receiving com-prehensive preventive services under EPSDT.	$1 spent on comprehensive prenatal care saves $3.38; annual health care costs are 10 percent lower for children receiving EPSDT services.
Childhood immunization program protects our children against preventable diseases.	Immunization rates generally fell in the early 1980s. For several groups and types of vaccine they have fallen below 80 percent.	Dramatic declines in the incidence of rubella, mumps, polio, diphtheria, tetanus, and pertussis; reduction in consequent impairments and institutionalization.	$1 spent on the childhood immunization program saves $10 in later medical costs.

11

PROGRAM	SHORTFALL	PROGRAM BENEFIT FOR CHILDREN	COST SAVINGS
Quality child care help enables low-income families to pay their child care bills.	The primary form of child care help—Title XX—lost in 1981 its direction that states have quality standards and lost more than one-half of its money from 1977 to 1989.	The Dodd-Hawkins-Hatch bill would provide more supportive child care, more choices for more parents, and (through state standards) increased safety of child care for children who otherwise would be left untended or in potentially harmful arrangements. Child care also increases well-being of children through higher parental earnings and self-sufficiency.	Child care reimbursements cost the public a small fraction of what monthly welfare payments cost for a family without a working parent. In addition, employers and parents report less absenteeism and greater productivity if there is adequate child care.
Head Start gives disadvantaged youngsters a range of crucial services.	Head Start serves fewer than one in six eligible youngsters.	Increases school success and eventual employability.	$1 invested in quality pre-school educa-tion returns $4.75 because of lower costs for special education, public assist-ance, and crime.
Chapter 1 Compensatory Education gives extra educational help to disadvantaged children.	In 1987, Chapter 1 served about one-half of the children who needed remedial education.	Linked to achievement gains and maintenance of gains in reading and mathematics while in the program.	Investment of $600 for a child for one year of compensatory education can save $4,000 in the cost of a single repeated grade.

PROGRAM	SHORTFALL	PROGRAM BENEFIT FOR CHILDREN	COST SAVINGS
Education for All Handicapped Children opens doors to learning for disabled youngsters.	The federal government is not living up to its earlier commitment to share the costs.	Increases the number of students receiving services, increases availability of appropriate services, and results in services being provided in less restrictive settings.	Early educational intervention has saved school districts $1,560 per disabled pupil.
Minimum wage increase (restoring the minimum wage to a level which allows a full-time worker to support at least a small family).	In 1991, after scheduled increases take effect, a worker employed full-time, year-round at the minimum wage still will earn less than 90 percent of a poverty-level income for a family of three.	Increases parental earnings and financial incentives to work, provides adequate economic base to support children.	Reduced expenditures for income support programs targeted on low-income families; increased personal income and payroll tax revenues associated with increased employment and earnings.
Youth employment and training and the Job Corps help prepare disadvantaged young people for the world of work.	Currently only 3 percent of the 1.2 million teenagers officially counted as unemployed are served.	Brings about gains in future employability and earnings for teenagers and young adults.	Every $1 invested in Job Corps yields $1.45 in benefits to American society. Other youth employment and training programs have raised post-program employment rates by nearly one-fourth and annual earnings by more than $1,300 per participant.

Investment Priorities for 1990

CHILD CARE
- Enact Dodd/Hawkins/Hatch legislation plus supplemental tax credits for low-income families.
- Increase state appropriations for child care; adopt state quality assurances.

HEAD START
- Reauthorize at a level sufficient to serve all eligible children and assure program quality.
- Increase state support levels for Head Start and other comprehensive preschool programs.

HEALTH AND NUTRITION
- Provide adequate funding to fully immunize all children.
- Extend Medicaid coverage to all pregnant women and children with family incomes below 200 percent of poverty level.
- Expand WIC to eliminate unmet need.
- States should fully utilize all federal funds for these programs and supplement as necessary to eliminate unmet need by 1994.

In addition to a sound child care bill, in 1990 the successful Head Start program must be reauthorized and expanded to a level sufficient to assure that no eligible children are turned away. Health and nutrition coverage should be extended to all mothers and children in families with incomes below twice the federal poverty level.

States need not wait for the federal government to act. Significant state dollars and implementation efforts should be directed to these same successful children's programs. But if we are to survive as a nation, it is vital that we not leave basic child protections to the political or economic fortunes of any state. States will always differ in their capacity to meet the needs of children, and a child's well-being should not depend on his or her residence.

Priorities for 1990-1992

In 1990 we also can lay the groundwork for advances for children in other critical areas:

Education and Youth Employment
- Establish high achievement and graduation goals for all students; increase resources and focus on schools and students that need extra help to meet those goals.

17

- Increase financial assistance for low-income college students.
- Increase high-quality after-school and summer programs for school-age children.

Employment Training
- Expand job training, apprenticeship, and community service programs that equip young adults with job skills.

Housing
- Expand programs that increase housing supply and provide subsidies for low-income families.

Health
- Expand programs that increase the supply of health care services for underserved communities.

Family Support
- Increase investments in programs that provide preventive and supportive services for families, reduce the incidence of child abuse and neglect, and reduce unnecessary out-of-home placement.

Income Support
- Ensure a living family wage and income supplements for low-income families.

The Very Affordable Cost of Eliminating Poverty

At a time when future demographic trends guarantee a shortage of young adults who will be workers, soldiers, leaders, and parents, America cannot afford to waste a single child, not even the poorest one. Poor children are more likely to die in infancy and childhood, be left disabled for life by preventable causes, lack basic reading and math skills, drop out of school, be unemployed, become pregnant as teenagers, and be dependent on welfare.

The federal government counts the number of poor people in the country and the amount by which their incomes fall below the poverty line. So we know what it would cost to eliminate poverty. Based on 1988 figures:

- Eliminating poverty in families with children would cost $26.1 billion.
- Eliminating poverty among all persons would cost $53.8 billion.

This sounds like a lot of money. And it is. But this is also a large and wealthy country. The cost of eliminating all poverty ($53.8 billion) is equivalent to only 1 percent of our gross national product. Eliminating poverty in families with children ($26.1 billion) would cost about 1.5 cents of every dollar federal, state, and local governments spend.

We can save our children—and our future—but only by making hard national choices and reordering our national investment priorities. The issue is not money but national will and values.

If bankers can get $164 billion to bail out deregulated, imprudent savings and loan institutions, and if we can afford the $5 billion in tax breaks for inherited capital

- Eliminate all child poverty.
- Close gaps in school achievement based on racial, economic, and other factors unrelated to ability.

gains for the wealthy, then this nation can afford to lift its 12 million poor children out of poverty. Similarly, if states can afford to spend $27,010 per year to keep a juvenile in custody, if they can spend $57,600 per cell in building new maximum security prisons, and if they can spend billions subsidizing shopping malls and government-operated liquor stores, then they can afford to invest in children. States ran a nearly $11 billion surplus in fiscal year 1990.

In a December 17, 1989, *Washington Post* article, *The Costs of Leadership,* former Federal Reserve Chair Paul Volcker wrote that America surely can afford to meet its pressing domestic needs: "It's a question of attitude, not of economics. You can afford what you think you really need—within limits. And I don't think we've reached those limits."

The Purposes of this Book

This briefing book is designed for all those in public life, child advocates, community activists, professionals, policymakers, parents, citizens, members of the media, and political leaders of all parties and their staffs. Its purpose is to dramatically increase public consciousness about children's needs and some solutions to those needs. Children cannot vote, lobby, or make campaign contributions. But parents, day care workers, pediatricians, members of religious congregations, minority group activists, and women—in short, every citizen 18 or older—can.

Our intent is not to influence any candidate's election. It is to use the election year process to build greater bipartisan commitment to meeting children's needs and to begin to reverse the perverse values and budget priorities of the 1980s that have contributed to mounting child suffering and neglect, the growing chasm between rich and poor, the decline of the middle class, and the weakening of the moral and social fabric that makes us Americans.

The history of the 1980s already is written. It will say:

- In the 1980s, 2.1 million children fell into poverty while the number of American billionaires quintupled between 1982 and 1989.
- The gap between rich and poor and the rich and the middle class grew. In 1960 corporate chief executive officers earned 41 times what factory workers made. By 1988 they earned 93 times factory workers' salaries. Almost twice a week the CEO got a check equal to the factory worker's annual salary. In the same period, a CEO's salary went from 38 times to 72 times the salary of a school teacher.
- The United States engaged in the largest military build-up in peacetime

history. Between 1980 and 1988 this country invested $1.9 trillion in national defense while cutting $10 billion from programs to defend poor children and families.

If we act now with dispatch and resolve, the history of the 1990s can say:

- In the 1990s America came to its senses. Child poverty was wiped out. And through positive leadership, vision, hard work, and systematic investment in proven strategies, gaps separating minority and poor children from other young Americans were eliminated. As a result, America faced the twenty-first century world with its ideals intact—showing the world through example that all God's children are precious.

Part II:
Children
in the Nation

INTERNATIONAL REPORT CARD

•

TWELVE BASIC FACTS ABOUT AMERICA'S CHILDREN

•

AN AMERICAN CHILD'S CHANCES OF BEING POOR

INTERNATIONAL

Report Card

U.S. Performance: Unsatisfactory

The United States ranks second in the world in per capita gross national product, but does not rank even in the top 10 in any of these measures that are crucial to children's health and well-being:

Children's Status	U.S. Rank
Infant mortality rate (1988) In the United States 10 babies died for every 1,000 live births. The United States ranked behind 18 other nations, including Singapore, Hong Kong, Spain, and Ireland.	19
Mortality rate for children younger than five (1988) In the United States, 13 of 1,000 babies died before their fifth birthdays. This ranks us twenty-second behind a list of countries that includes Japan, Singapore, New Zealand, and East Germany.	22
Low-birthweight births (1988) In the United States, 7 percent of babies were born at low birthweight. Twenty-eight countries, including Austria, Hong Kong, and both East and West Germany, did better.	29

Children's Status	U.S. Rank
Proportion of one-year-olds fully immunized against polio (latest reported year) While 95 percent of U.S. one-year-olds were immunized, 14 nations had better rates. Moreover, when the U.S. *nonwhite* population's rate (82 percent of one-year-olds fully immunized against polio) is compared with other nations' overall rates, the United States lags behind 48 other countries, including Albania, Oman, Botswana, Tunisia, and Sri Lanka.	15
Number of school-age children per teacher (1986) The United States ratio (23-to-one) lagged behind 18 countries, including, Libya, East Germany, Lebanon, and Cuba, and tied Malta and Kuwait.	19
Childhood poverty (1979-1982) The United States was last, behind Switzerland, Sweden, Norway, West Germany, Canada, the United Kingdom, and Australia. The U.S. child poverty rate (17.1 percent) was two to three times higher than those of most of the other countries studied.	8 (among eight industrialized countries)
Mathematical achievement of eighth-grade students (1981-1982) U.S. students' test scores were lower than those of students in Japan, Hungary, England, and eight other countries.	12 (among 18 selected nations)
Expenditures on public education as a percentage of the gross national product (1983) The United States' spending of 5.6 percent of GNP was behind such nations as Italy, Hungary, and Canada.	7 (among 14 selected countries)
Teen pregnancy rates (1985) U.S. teenage pregnancy rates were higher than those for teenage women in Canada, England and Wales, France, the Netherlands, and Sweden.	6 (among six selected nations)

Investments in Children	Yes/No	
Is the United States one of 70 nations worldwide that provide medical care and financial assistance to all pregnant women?	☐	☑
Is the United States one of 61 nations around the world that insure or provide basic medical care to all workers and their dependents?	☐	☑
Is the United States one of 63 nations worldwide that provide a family allowance to workers and their children?	☐	☑
Is the United States one of 17 industrialized nations that have paid maternity/parenting leave programs?	☐	☑

On November 20, 1989 the United Nations General Assembly unanimously approved a groundbreaking international Convention on the Rights of the Child. The convention spells out critical economic, social, cultural, civil, and political rights of children. If the United States ratifies the convention, it would confront this nation with the necessity of remedying many of the problems its children face and improving on its wholly unsatisfactory rating on this report card. Combined with the plans of the U.N. to hold the first world Children's Summit of heads of state in September 1990, the convention offers new hope for a new world ethic placing greater value on children's survival and well-being.

America's Children

Every citizen, every public official, every civil servant and officeholder, every reporter, and every candidate should know the basic facts about America's children and understand how the problems revealed in those facts endanger America's children and the nation's future.

1. Because of demographic changes, America faces a future in which children and young workers will be a shrinking share of the population. *In the year 2000 there will be 4.1 million fewer Americans in the young adult age group (18 to 24) entering the work force than there were in the mid-1980s, a decline of 14 percent.*

2. A growing share of this shrinking work force will be minority. *In the year 2000 nearly one-third of the nation's 18- to 24-year-olds will be from minority groups, compared with less than one-quarter in 1985.*

3. While we will need every individual in this shrinking future work force to be a productive worker, we are subverting the attainment of that goal by consigning a growing number of children to poverty. *Between 1979 and 1988 the proportion of American children living in poverty grew by 23 percent. One in five American children lives in poverty.* If recent trends continue, by the year 2000 one in four will be living in poverty.

4. American children's health and development is threatened as well by lack of health insurance and lack of access to health care. *More than 12 million children and more than 14 million women of childbearing age have no health insurance.*

5. The lack of access to health care is reflected in the worsening or stagnation during the 1980s of many key health indicators. *After many years of substantial progress, our nation's improvement in the rates of early prenatal care, low-birthweight births, and infant mortality has slowed down dramatically or stopped. Immunization rates actually have declined. The United States has slipped to nineteenth in the world in preventing infant deaths,* behind such nations as Spain, Ireland, Hong Kong, and Singapore.

6. The earnings of men younger than 30 have dropped sharply since 1973. When young men make very low wages, young couples are far less likely to get married. *Since 1973 young men's marriage rates have declined by one-third, and the proportion of births that were out of wedlock doubled.* As young workers' earnings declined and more single-parent families developed, median incomes for young families with children dropped by 24 percent from 1973 to 1987, even though many more women entered the work force. Just 29 percent of American children now live in "traditional" families in which fathers work for wages and mothers care for children at home.

7. *One-half of preschool-age children today have mothers employed outside the home. By the year 2000 that figure will rise to nearly seven in 10. But our nation barely has begun to adapt to the dramatically expanding need for safe, accessible, affordable child care.* Head Start serves fewer than one in six eligible children, and the other longstanding source of direct child care assistance for poor families, Title XX, in 1981 lost its direction that states have quality standards. Title XX also has withered in scope over the past dozen years (it now is funded at levels less than half those of 1977, adjusted for inflation), while the number of preschool children in poverty soared.

8. Our schools are failing. Many of them, and especially those serving poor and minority children, are simply not good enough to prepare our children for the demands of the twenty-first century. *One-half million children drop out of school in the United States each year.* Poor teenagers are three times more likely than other teens to drop out and are four times more likely to have below-average basic skills.

9. Between 1979 and 1986 there was a 66 percent increase in the reported number of cases in which children were endangered by abuse or neglect. *In 1986, 2.2 million children were reported abused, neglected, or both.*

10. The fastest growing segment of the homeless population in America is families with children. *Every night an estimated 100,000 children go to sleep homeless.* The National Conference of Mayors reports that one in four homeless people in their cities is a child.

11. The U.S. teen pregnancy rate is twice as high as that of other industrialized countries. *Two in every five American girls get pregnant and one in every five American girls bears a child before the age of 20.* The vast majority aren't married. Much of this has to do with poverty and lack of achievement: regardless of race, teens with below-average academic skills and from poor families are about five to seven times more likely to be parents than are teens with solid skills and from nonpoor families.

12. As families with children have struggled against this rising tide of poverty, out-of-wedlock births, single parenthood, lack of health insurance, homelessness and bad housing, lack of quality child care, and inadequate schools, many sources of public help, especially at the national level, have shrunk. *Low-income housing assistance is down 76 percent (adjusted for inflation) since 1980; federal help for elementary and secondary education is down 22.4 percent from 1979; the AFDC grant for subsistence in a median state has fallen by 37 percent since 1970; and the main federal program to place doctors in underserved areas of the country has lost more than 90 percent of its doctors.*

AN AMERICAN CHILD'S

Chances
OF BEING
Poor

If white	1 in 7
If black	4 in 9
If Hispanic	3 in 8
If in a female-headed family	1 in 2
If younger than three	1 in 4
If three to five	2 in 9
If six to 17	2 in 11
If the child is also a parent	7 in 10
If the family head is younger than 25	1 in 2
If the family head is younger than 30	1 in 3

Part III: Children in the States

STATE REPORT CARD

•

KEY NUMBERS ON CHILDREN IN THE STATES

•

CHILD CARE IN THE STATES

STATE

Report Card

The Children's Defense Fund measured trends in children's well-being in every state over the past decade and the adequacy of states' efforts to improve children's lives. Armed with these data, citizens, media, elected officials, and candidates are in a better position to identify the most serious problems in their states, and to set priorities for the 1990s. There are two parts to the Report Card:

- Adequacy of state progress on 10 key indicators of children's well-being;
- Adequacy of state investments in 10 key programs of importance to children and families.

The Report Card shows how each state and the District of Columbia scored on each of the 20 performance measures and shows how many received credit on each indicator. In the Appendix 20 tables—one for each indicator—detail how the scores were arrived at for each state.

Trends in Children's Well-Being

Three states—Alabama, New Hampshire, and Vermont—demonstrated adequate progress on six or more of the 10 measures of children's well-being. Arizona and Maryland ranked the worst, showing stagnation, deterioration, or inadequate progress in nine out of the 10 measures.

Key Findings

1. **Early Prenatal Care:** Infants born to women who receive early and comprehensive prenatal care are far less likely to die in the first year or be left disabled for life. Yet *no state* has improved the provision of prenatal care to

---

NOTE: Individual state fact sheets, summarizing how each state and the District of Columbia compared with the national average or the definition of adequate progress or investments in children, are available from the Children's Defense Fund.

STATE REPORT CARD

The Adequacy* of States' Progress in Improving Children's Status During the 1980s

		(1) Pre- natal Care	(2) Infant Mort- ality	(3) Low Birth weight	(4) Teen Birth- Rate	(5) Births to Un- married	(6) Paternities Estab- lished	(7) Child Pover- ty	(8) Housing Afford- ability	(9) High School Grad.	(10) Youth Unemp- ment	Sub- total
U.S. Total	Yes:	0	30	5	34	22	23	2	1	29	25	—
	No:	50	21	46	16	29	27	49	50	22	26	—
Not Available:		1	–	–	1	–	1	–	–	–	–	
Alabama		No	No	No	Yes	Yes	Yes	No	Yes	Yes	Yes	6
Alaska		No	No	Yes	Yes	No	Yes	No	No	Yes	No	4
Arizona		No	Yes	No	No	No	No	No	No	No	No	1
Arkansas		No	Yes	No	Yes	Yes	Yes	No	No	Yes	No	5
California		No	Yes	No	No	Yes	No	No	No	Yes	No	3
Colorado		No	No	No	Yes	No	No	No	No	Yes	No	2
Connecticut		No	Yes	No	No	Yes	No	No	No	Yes	Yes	4
Delaware		No	No	No	No	Yes	Yes	Yes	No	Yes	Yes	5
District of Columbia		No	No	No	n/a	Yes	No	No	No	No	Yes	2
Florida		No	No	No	No	Yes	Yes	No	No	No	Yes	3
Georgia		No	No	No	Yes	Yes	Yes	No	No	No	No	3
Hawaii		No	Yes	No	Yes	Yes	No	No	No	No	Yes	4
Idaho		No	No	No	Yes	No	Yes	No	No	Yes	No	3
Illinois		No	No	No	Yes	Yes	Yes	No	No	No	No	3
Indiana		No	No	No	Yes	No	Yes	No	No	Yes	Yes	4
Iowa		No	Yes	No	Yes	No	No	No	No	Yes	No	3
Kansas		No	Yes	No	Yes	No	No	No	No	No	No	2
Kentucky		No	Yes	No	Yes	No	Yes	No	No	Yes	No	4
Louisiana		No	No	No	Yes	No	No	No	No	Yes	No	2
Maine		No	Yes	No	Yes	No	Yes	No	No	Yes	Yes	5
Maryland		No	No	No	No	Yes	No	No	No	No	No	1
Massachusetts		No	Yes	No	No	Yes	Yes	No	No	No	Yes	4
Michigan		No	No	No	No	Yes	Yes	No	No	No	Yes	3
Minnesota		No	Yes	Yes	Yes	No	No	No	No	Yes	No	4
Mississippi		No	No	No	Yes	Yes	No	No	No	Yes	No	3
Missouri		No	Yes	No	Yes	No	n/a	No	No	No	No	2
Montana		No	No	No	Yes	No	Yes	No	No	Yes	No	3
Nebraska		No	Yes	No	Yes	No	Yes	No	No	Yes	No	4
Nevada		No	Yes	No	No	Yes	No	No	No	Yes	Yes	4
New Hampshire		No	Yes	Yes	Yes	No	Yes	Yes	No	No	Yes	6
New Jersey		No	Yes	No	No	Yes	No	No	No	No	Yes	3
New Mexico		n/a	Yes	No	No	No	No	No	No	Yes	No	2
New York		No	No	No	No	Yes	No	No	No	No	Yes	2
North Carolina		No	No	No	No	Yes	No	No	No	No	Yes	2
North Dakota		No	Yes	Yes	Yes	No	Yes	No	No	Yes	No	5
Ohio		No	Yes	No	Yes	No	No	No	No	Yes	Yes	4
Oklahoma		No	Yes	No	Yes	No	No	No	No	Yes	No	3
Oregon		No	No	Yes	Yes	No	No	No	No	No	Yes	2
Pennsylvania		No	No	No	No	No	Yes	No	No	Yes	Yes	3
Rhode Island		No	Yes	No	No	No	No	No	No	No	Yes	2
South Carolina		No	No	No	Yes	Yes	Yes	No	No	Yes	Yes	5
South Dakota		No	Yes	No	Yes	No	Yes	No	No	No	No	3
Tennessee		No	No	No	Yes	Yes	No	No	No	No	Yes	3
Texas		No	Yes	No	Yes	No	No	No	No	Yes	No	3
Utah		No	Yes	No	Yes	No	No	No	No	Yes	Yes	4
Vermont		No	Yes	Yes	Yes	Yes	Yes	No	No	No	Yes	6
Virginia		No	Yes	No	Yes	Yes	No	No	No	No	Yes	4
Washington		No	Yes	No	Yes	No	Yes	No	No	No	No	3
West Virginia		No	Yes	No	Yes	No	No	No	No	Yes	No	3
Wisconsin		No	Yes	No	No	No	Yes	No	No	Yes	Yes	4
Wyoming		No	Yes	No	Yes	No	No	No	No	Yes	No	3

*The definitions of adequate progress, used to award credit for each measure, are explained in the Appendix.

n/a = not available.

The Adequacy* of State Program Investments for Children

(11) (12) Medicaid Coverage		(13) Nutri-tion Assistance	(14) Early Educ. Efforts	(15) Child Care Qual.	(16) Child Support Enforc.	(17) AFDC In-creases	(18) Rent vs. AFDC	(19) Stdt.-Teacher Ratio	(20) Youth Emp. Efforts	Sub-total	TOTAL SCORE	
Preg.Women & Babies	Child-ren										Number	Percent
15	17	10	29	30	19	2	0	8	28	–		32%
36	34	41	22	20	30	49	51	43	23	–	(U.S. Avg.)	
—	—	—	—	1	2	—	—	—	—	–		
No	No	No	No	No	Yes	No	No	No	No	1	7	35%
No	No	Yes	Yes	No	No	No	No	No	Yes	3	7	35
No	Yes	No	No	No	Yes	No	No	No	Yes	3	4	20
No	Yes	No	No	No	No	No	No	No	No	1	6	30
Yes	Yes	No	Yes	Yes	No	Yes	No	No	Yes	6	9	45
No	No	No	No	No	No	No	No	No	Yes	1	3	15
Yes	No	No	Yes	Yes	Yes	No	No	Yes	Yes	6	10	50
No	No	Yes	Yes	Yes	Yes	No	No	No	Yes	5	10	50
No	No	Yes	Yes	No	No	No	No	Yes	No	3	5	25
No	Yes	No	Yes	No	No	No	No	No	Yes	3	6	30
No	No	No	No	No	No	No	No	No	Yes	1	4	20
Yes	No	No	Yes	n/a	No	No	No	No	No	2	6	30
No	No	No	No	No	No	No	No	No	No	0	3	15
No	No	Yes	Yes	Yes	Yes	No	No	No	Yes	5	8	40
No	No	No	No	Yes	n/a	No	No	No	No	1	5	25
Yes	Yes	No	No	Yes	No	No	No	No	Yes	4	7	35
No	No	No	No	Yes	No	No	No	No	No	1	3	15
No	No	No	Yes	No	No	No	No	No	No	1	5	25
No	Yes	No	Yes	No	Yes	No	No	No	No	3	5	25
Yes	Yes	No	Yes	Yes	No	Yes	No	Yes	Yes	7	12	60
Yes	No	No	Yes	Yes	Yes	No	No	No	Yes	5	6	30
Yes	No	Yes	Yes	Yes	Yes	No	No	Yes	Yes	7	11	55
Yes	No	No	Yes	Yes	No	No	No	No	Yes	4	7	35
Yes	Yes	Yes	Yes	Yes	Yes	No	No	No	Yes	7	11	55
Yes	No	No	No	No	No	No	No	No	No	1	4	20
No	No	No	Yes	Yes	No	No	No	No	No	2	4	20
No	No	No	No	Yes	No	No	No	No	Yes	2	5	25
No	No	No	No	Yes	No	No	No	No	No	1	5	25
No	Yes	No	No	Yes	No	No	No	No	No	2	6	30
No	No	No	No	Yes	No	No	No	No	Yes	2	8	40
No	No	No	Yes	Yes	Yes	No	No	Yes	Yes	5	8	40
No	No	No	No	No	No	No	No	No	No	0	2	10
Yes	No	Yes	Yes	Yes	Yes	No	No	No	Yes	6	8	40
No	Yes	No	No	No	Yes	No	No	No	Yes	3	5	25
No	No	No	No	Yes	Yes	No	No	No	No	2	7	35
No	No	No	Yes	No	No	No	No	No	Yes	2	6	30
No	No	No	Yes	Yes	No	AFDC	No	Stdt.-	No	2	5	25
No	No	No	Yes	Yes	No	In-	No	No	Yes	3	5	25
No	No	Yes	Efforts	Yes	Yes	creases	AFDC	Ratio	Yes	5	8	40
Yes	Yes	No	Yes	Yes	Yes	No	No	Yes	No	6	8	40
Yes	Yes	No	Yes	No	Yes	No	No	No	No	4	9	45
No	No	No	No	No	No	No	No	No	No	0	3	15
No	Yes	No	No	No	Yes	No	No	No	Yes	3	6	30
No	No	Yes	Yes	No	No	No	No	No	No	2	5	25
No	No	No	No	Yes	No	No	No	No	No	1	5	25
Yes	Yes	No	Yes	Yes	Yes	No	No	Yes	Yes	7	13	65
No	No	No	No	Yes	Yes	No	No	No	Yes	3	7	35
Yes	Yes	No	Yes	Yes	No	No	No	No	Yes	5	8	40
No	Yes	No	Yes	Yes	No	No	No	No	No	3	6	30
No	No	Yes	Yes	Yes	n/a	No	No	No	Yes	4	8	40
No	Yes	No	No	No	No	No	No	Yes	No	2	5	25

*The definitions of adequate program investment, used to award credit for each measure, are explained in the Appendix.

n/a = not applicable or not available.

pregnant women at a rate fast enough to meet the U.S. Surgeon General's goal of ensuring that, by 1990, 90 percent of all pregnant women begin receiving care in the first three months of pregnancy.

2. **Infant Mortality:** Only *30 states* have made enough progress in reducing infant deaths so that they meet or can be expected to meet by 1990 the U.S. Surgeon General's goal of no more than nine deaths per 1,000 live births.

3. **Low-Birthweight Births:** Babies born at low birthweight are 20 times more likely to die in infancy and are at greater risk of being born with lifelong disabilities. But only *five states* have made enough progress in reducing the proportion of infants born at low birthweight to meet the U.S. Surgeon General's 1990 low-birthweight goal of 5 percent.

4. **Births to Teens:** *Thirty-four states* have done better than the national average in the percentage of decline in births to teenage girls ages 15 to 19.

5. **Births to Unmarried Women:** The percent of births to unmarried women has risen in every state, although *21 states and the District of Columbia* had rates of increase less than the national average.

6. **Paternities Established:** As the proportion of births to unmarried mothers rises, the need to establish paternity for purposes of child support and other benefits increases. *Twenty-three states* have increased the number of paternities established per births to unmarried women at rates faster than the national average.

7. **Children in Poverty:** Between 1979 and 1985 the proportion of children living in poverty grew by 25 percent. In all but *two states*—Delaware and New Hampshire—the percent of children living in poverty increased from 1979 to 1985.

8. **Affordability of Housing for the Poor:** One of the biggest threats to children's well-being is poor families' increasing inability to secure safe, affordable housing. Housing experts and the U.S. Department of Housing and Urban Development recommend that families pay no more than 30 percent of their monthly income for housing costs. But in every state *except one* (Alabama) the fair market rental price for a two-bedroom apartment in the state's most affordable metropolitan area exceeded 30 percent of the federal poverty level for a family of four.

9. **High School Graduation:** Without basic academic training and at least a high school diploma, young people are at a huge disadvantage in the increasingly competitive job market. High school graduation rates improved gradually over the past decade and *29 states* have raised the percentage of ninth-graders who graduate four years later at a rate that exceeds the national rate of improvement.

10. **Youth Unemployment:** *Twenty-four states and the District of Columbia* saw declines in youth unemployment at rates that exceeded the national rate of decline between 1982 and 1988. In five states youth unemployment actually increased during this time.

State Investments in Children's Programs

Five states (Iowa, Maine, Massachusetts, Minnesota, and Vermont) made sufficient investments in seven of the 10 program areas. Three states (Idaho, New Mexico, and South Dakota) are not making sufficient investments for children in any category.

Key Findings

11. Medicaid Coverage of Babies and Pregnant Women: Despite the strong relationship between access to health care during pregnancy and infancy and the health of mothers and children, only *15 states* provided Medicaid coverage in late 1989 to the full extent that the federal program would fund with federal dollars (for all pregnant women and infants younger than one with family incomes less than 185 percent of the federal poverty level).

12. Medicaid Coverage of Poor Children: In 1989 federal law permitted states to provide Medicaid coverage to all children younger than six with family incomes below the federal poverty level. But by the end of 1989 only one-third of the states *(17 states)* did so. (A new law will *require* states to do so by April 1990.)

13. Nutritional Assistance for Mothers and Children: Despite the proven effectiveness of the Special Supplemental Food Program for Women, Infants, and Children (WIC) in improving maternal and child health and its dramatic cost effectiveness, only *nine states and the District of Columbia* supplement their federal WIC allotment to provide food and nutrition services to additional pregnant women, infants, and children beyond those covered by the federal allotment. (Federal WIC funds reach slightly more than half of all eligible women and children.)

14. Support for Early Childhood Education: Only *28 states and the District of Columbia* invest their own funds in Head Start or other early childhood education programs, despite the proven effectiveness of such programs in reducing subsequent school failure, dropout, and lifetime dependency. Federal Head Start funds reach only one in six eligible children.

15. Child Care Quality: Infant-to-Staff Ratio: Because federal funding for child care is so inadequate, states must invest substantially if the urgent need for safe, affordable, and high quality care among lower income working families is to be met. In addition, states have the prime responsibility for assuring the safety and quality of child care arrangements. Yet only *29 states and the District of Columbia* have infant-to-worker staffing requirements that meet the four-to-one ratio recommended by the National Association for the Education of Young Children.

16. State Child Support Enforcement Efforts: One reason for the large percentage of children living in poverty is that, too frequently, children with absent parents are denied support or paid hopelessly inadequate amounts. *Nineteen states* exceeded the national average in 1988 in collecting child support award amounts owed.

35

17. Changes in Public Assistance Benefits Compared with Inflation: For families that must rely on public assistance, the monthly AFDC benefit levels in effect during 1989 did not come close to reflecting the real costs of food, housing, clothes, and other essentials. Actual benefit levels for a family of three ranged from 84 percent of the federal poverty line to as little as 15 percent. One reason benefits are so low is that they have lagged far behind inflation. Only *two states* kept AFDC benefits in line with inflation from 1970 to 1989.

18. Adequacy of AFDC Benefits in Relation to Housing Costs: Families with children are the fastest growing segment of the homeless population. Those at greatest risk of homelessness are families that depend on public assistance. The federal government recommends that a family spend no more than 30 percent of its monthly income on housing. Yet in *no state* are housing costs for apartments in the most affordable metropolitan region 30 percent or less of the monthly AFDC benefit. In two-thirds of the states (38) the cost of the lowest priced rental unit actually exceeds a family's entire monthly AFDC payment, leaving most families in substandard housing or without any housing at all.

19. Student-to-Teacher Ratio: Smaller classes and individualized attention help children, particularly those who are low-income or minority, achieve at higher levels. But by 1988 only *seven states and the District of Columbia* had class sizes of 15 or fewer students per classroom teacher, as recommended by professional education organizations.

20. State Youth Employment Initiatives: Despite the effectiveness of job creation and training efforts in assisting employment readiness, only *28 states* supplement inadequate federal funding levels for youth employment programs.

	Estimated Number of Children Under Age 5 (1987)	Estimated Number of Children Under 18 (1987)	Estimated Total State Population (1987)	Estimated Average Number of Poor Children (1983-1987)	Estimated Average Percent of Poor Children (1983-1987)
United States Total	18,252,000	63,542,000	243,400,000	13,055,000	20.9%
Alabama	295,000	1,117,000	4,083,000	358,000	31.7
Alaska	60,000	171,000	525,000	21,000	12.7
Arizona	287,000	919,000	3,386,000	183,000	21.2
Arkansas	173,000	647,000	2,388,000	192,000	29.0
California	2,302,000	7,301,000	27,663,000	1,512,000	21.4
Colorado	268,000	874,000	3,296,000	131,000	16.2
Connecticut	214,000	757,000	3,211,000	86,000	11.8
Delaware	47,000	162,000	644,000	24,000	15.3
District of Columbia	46,000	136,000	622,000	39,000	31.3
Florida	812,000	2,704,000	12,023,000	575,000	21.1
Georgia	477,000	1,736,000	6,222,000	381,000	24.2
Hawaii	89,000	286,000	1,083,000	46,000	16.7
Idaho	84,000	305,000	998,000	67,000	21.7
Illinois	861,000	3,035,000	11,582,000	730,000	22.8
Indiana	390,000	1,470,000	5,531,000	259,000	18.4
Iowa	196,000	732,000	2,834,000	170,000	21.3
Kansas	192,000	651,000	2,476,000	96,000	14.5
Kentucky	258,000	996,000	3,727,000	238,000	23.6
Louisiana	385,000	1,316,000	4,461,000	390,000	30.6
Maine	83,000	303,000	1,187,000	48,000	16.0
Maryland	333,000	1,125,000	4,535,000	133,000	13.0
Massachusetts	389,000	1,336,000	5,855,000	204,000	14.1
Michigan	665,000	2,460,000	9,200,000	564,000	22.7
Minnesota	323,000	1,111,000	4,246,000	186,000	16.3
Mississippi	211,000	792,000	2,625,000	257,000	34.3
Missouri	369,000	1,309,000	5,103,000	268,000	20.5
Montana	64,000	224,000	809,000	48,000	20.1
Nebraska	122,000	423,000	1,594,000	86,000	18.7
Nevada	77,000	252,000	1,007,000	39,000	15.2
New Hampshire	76,000	266,000	1,057,000	15,000	6.2
New Jersey	513,000	1,831,000	7,672,000	288,000	15.5
New Mexico	134,000	447,000	1,500,000	117,000	27.5
New York	1,248,000	4,361,000	17,825,000	1,031,000	23.6
North Carolina	438,000	1,627,000	6,413,000	294,000	19.5
North Dakota	55,000	187,000	672,000	33,000	16.4
Ohio	773,000	2,837,000	10,784,000	581,000	20.2
Oklahoma	258,000	893,000	3,272,000	188,000	21.0
Oregon	190,000	686,000	2,724,000	121,000	17.7
Pennsylvania	783,000	2,851,000	11,936,000	516,000	18.4
Rhode Island	65,000	229,000	986,000	38,000	16.7
South Carolina	256,000	941,000	3,425,000	215,000	23.5
South Dakota	58,000	196,000	709,000	43,000	21.3
Tennessee	328,000	1,251,000	4,855,000	293,000	25.2
Texas	1,502,000	4,984,000	16,789,000	1,079,000	23.3
Utah	184,000	629,000	1,680,000	81,000	13.2
Vermont	40,000	140,000	548,000	22,000	16.1
Virginia	421,000	1,460,000	5,904,000	207,000	14.9
Washington	342,000	1,169,000	4,538,000	194,000	16.9
West Virginia	117,000	490,000	1,897,000	155,000	30.4
Wisconsin	356,000	1,270,000	4,807,000	199,000	15.8
Wyoming	43,000	148,000	490,000	23,000	15.5

Child Care in the States

	Percent of Children in Single-Parent Families (1980)	No. of Mothers in Labor Force who Have Children Under 6 (1980)	Percent of Mothers of Children Under 6 who Are in the Labor Force (1980)	No. of Mothers in Labor Force who Have Children Age 6-17 (1980)	Percent of Mothers of Children Age 6-17 who Are in the Labor Force (1980)	Title XX-Funded Child Care Slots (1988)
United States Total	23.3%	6,220,525	45.68%	10,726,125	63.03%	n/a
Alabama	27.0	121,144	48.97	185,976	60.74	6,500
Alaska	20.1	14,815	47.37	19,010	65.29	6,093
Arizona	22.4	74,582	44.54	116,676	61.40	14,945
Arkansas	24.4	74,852	50.99	109,235	62.59	2,191
California	26.1	643,658	46.34	1,084,702	65.16	112,500
Colorado	20.2	84,877	46.37	143,495	66.14	8,191
Connecticut	21.4	65,531	40.85	165,479	66.68	12,000
Delaware	25.0	16,777	48.76	30,835	64.96	1,976
District of Columbia	58.4	16,814	62.13	28,153	72.15	6,739
Florida	28.5	239,124	50.70	438,971	64.86	34,534
Georgia	28.5	187,672	53.94	290,484	66.56	7,999
Hawaii	21.9	32,215	51.46	45,523	69.65	1,188
Idaho	16.0	30,658	43.47	42,557	64.53	1,057
Illinois	24.2	299,384	43.35	533,822	63.19	20,528
Indiana	20.2	166,157	47.10	276,698	64.05	7,000
Iowa	14.8	90,190	49.13	140,500	65.80	1,673
Kansas	17.5	72,676	48.31	114,595	67.31	5,458
Kentucky	20.8	103,395	41.95	159,815	55.82	7,714
Louisiana	28.6	128,005	43.98	173,225	55.54	6,500
Maine	19.4	30,097	45.34	56,765	63.62	2,400
Maryland	27.0	117,155	50.85	233,397	66.86	8,745
Massachusetts	21.6	121,355	41.82	281,921	65.45	18,451
Michigan	23.6	238,178	41.58	437,667	59.59	7,539
Minnesota	14.6	127,727	50.38	205,757	66.97	n/a
Mississippi	30.9	92,586	54.40	117,569	62.78	2,712
Missouri	21.7	151,162	50.53	235,719	64.36	8,969
Montana	17.0	23,679	44.65	36,461	63.35	455
Nebraska	15.8	50,622	49.36	74,200	67.18	14,784
Nevada	26.0	24,364	54.13	41,651	71.13	280
New Hampshire	17.3	26,858	49.73	50,486	70.02	6,500
New Jersey	23.8	155,381	39.11	360,544	62.21	13,500
New Mexico	23.0	39,715	42.50	55,396	57.21	3,400
New York	26.9	359,593	37.50	776,996	59.28	6,200
North Carolina	26.0	203,233	58.32	335,633	70.34	15,300
North Dakota	12.3	21,173	47.23	26,499	58.99	190
Ohio	20.6	280,855	42.17	498,759	59.28	15,800
Oklahoma	20.9	93,784	47.20	143,290	63.21	15,500
Oregon	21.6	69,430	43.14	123,183	64.54	4,981
Pennsylvania	20.8	237,285	37.39	514,559	57.44	26,823
Rhode Island	21.6	22,026	45.01	48,863	68.02	1,861
South Carolina	28.3	114,638	58.12	167,117	67.94	4,500
South Dakota	16.5	24,227	50.90	30,524	64.55	64
Tennessee	25.2	143,252	50.96	231,926	63.41	12,349
Texas	22.1	468,649	48.10	661,620	63.02	14,900
Utah	13.3	49,346	37.44	55,339	64.46	7,503
Vermont	18.8	14,469	48.10	26,246	67.59	2,200
Virginia	24.1	155,359	49.80	275,923	64.93	4,502
Washington	20.7	107,403	42.71	193,407	63.71	8,690
West Virginia	17.8	39,780	31.62	68,158	45.94	4,700
Wisconsin	16.9	139,824	48.59	239,384	67.34	12,690
Wyoming	15.6	14,794	41.53	21,415	66.57	1,336

the States

	Number of Infant Deaths (1987)	Number of Low-Birthweight Births (1987)	Number of Babies Born to Teens (1987)	Percent of All Births That Were to Teens (1987)
United States Total	38,408	262,344	472,623	12.4%
Alabama	727	4,788	10,359	17.4%
Alaska	121	564	1,085	9.3%
Arizona	601	4,084	8,781	13.9%
Arkansas	356	2,662	6,501	18.8%
California	4,546	30,328	54,599	10.8%
Colorado	527	4,264	5,718	10.6%
Connecticut	411	3,125	4,023	8.6%
Delaware	116	658	1,313	13.3%
District of Columbia	197	1,380	1,665	16.3%
Florida	1,848	13,423	23,664	13.5%
Georgia	1,306	8,446	17,009	16.6%
Hawaii	166	1,306	1,820	9.8%
Idaho	165	893	1,764	11.1%
Illinois	2,102	13,370	22,421	12.4%
Indiana	790	5,088	10,898	13.9%
Iowa	343	1,933	3,509	9.3%
Kansas	364	2,447	4,372	11.4%
Kentucky	499	3,494	8,866	17.3%
Louisiana	872	6,412	12,446	16.8%
Maine	139	902	1,784	10.6%
Maryland	831	5,656	8,284	11.4%
Massachusetts	611	4,812	7,038	8.3%
Michigan	1,508	10,058	17,247	12.3%
Minnesota	564	3,255	4,856	7.5%
Mississippi	566	3,701	8,304	20.1%
Missouri	769	5,240	10,018	13.3%
Montana	122	673	1,238	10.1%
Nebraska	204	1,308	2,121	8.9%
Nevada	160	1,150	1,953	11.7%
New Hampshire	132	839	1,323	7.8%
New Jersey	1,063	7,889	10,414	9.2%
New Mexico	221	1,919	4,172	15.3%
New York	2,906	20,568	25,616	9.4%
North Carolina	1,112	7,363	14,713	15.7%
North Dakota	90	503	786	7.6%
Ohio	1,461	10,364	20,823	13.2%
Oklahoma	458	3,216	7,676	16.0%
Oregon	403	2,077	4,425	11.4%
Pennsylvania	1,685	11,257	17,738	10.9%
Rhode Island	118	844	1,379	9.8%
South Carolina	673	4,529	8,676	16.4%
South Dakota	114	593	1,192	10.4%
Tennessee	795	5,530	11,426	16.8%
Texas	2,760	20,959	45,428	15.0%
Utah	312	2,026	3,342	9.5%
Vermont	69	427	649	8.0%
Virginia	923	6,256	10,279	11.4%
Washington	682	3,746	7,335	10.4%
West Virginia	219	1,591	3,819	17.0%
Wisconsin	612	3,850	6,912	9.7%
Wyoming	69	578	844	11.2%

Part IV:
Tools To Use

STEPS TO TAKE IN 1990

•

STEPS CDF WILL TAKE IN 1990

•

SCHEDULED CONGRESSIONAL RECESSES IN 1990

•

PROMISES TO REMEMBER

•

QUESTIONS TO ASK

•

POLLS TO CITE

•

CDF'S NONPARTISAN CONGRESSIONAL
VOTING RECORD OF 1989

Steps To Take

IN 1990

If you are a citizen, parent, or child advocate:

- **Immediately write or call** House Speaker Tom Foley (U.S. House of Representatives, Washington, D.C. 20515); Senate Majority Leader George Mitchell (U.S. Senate, Washington, D.C. 20510); and President Bush (Washington, D.C. 20500) and tell them to place investment in children at the top of their 1990 priorities, and that the bottom line of any child care bill should be a substantial investment in quality care—what's good for children and not just what's good for politicians.

- **Immediately write or call** your congressional representative (Washington, D.C. 20515) and U.S. senators (Washington, D.C. 20510), and tell them to place investment in children at the top of their 1990 priorities, including a substantial investment in quality child care. Visit their back-home offices (see recess schedule on page 49). Invite them to your children's program, congregation, or organizational meeting. Do your homework about the important differences for children in pending child care proposals. Ask them for specific commitments to invest in children in 1990, including child care.

- **Write your governor, state senator, and state representative** urging them to support well-conceived federal and state investments in children. Do your part in making sure programs for children are well implemented. Invite newly elected and incumbent local officials to a forum to hear about the problems of children in your community and to talk about how they intend to work with you to address those problems.

- **Attend town meetings. Take candidates to visit** neonatal intensive care nurseries, boarder baby wards, homeless shelters, decaying housing projects, custodial schools and day care programs, and juvenile institutions to see firsthand the unnecessary suffering and waste of precious child lives at enormous public cost. Educate them about the alternatives and how their votes and leadership can change these conditions.

45

- **Consider a stint of public service.** Run for public office at any level on a child investment platform. Think about what could happen if more people who were committed to children (rather than to their own careers) decided to serve in the legislative and executive branches at all levels for a few years.

- **Register and vote for children.** Too many officeholders do not see voteless, voiceless, and vulnerable children as important either to their own reelection or the nation's future. Children cannot vote, but you can. Yet tens of millions of Americans, including women, blacks, and Hispanics, are not using their voting power to improve the lives of children and families. In 1988:
  - Blacks of voting age used only 51.5 percent of their voting power;
  - Hispanic citizens used only 45.9 percent of their voting power;
  - Women used only 58.3 percent of their voting power; and
  - Fewer than four in 10 adults younger than 30 voted.

- **Encourage parents and members of your congregation and civic clubs to register and vote.** Voter registration campaigns should be conducted regularly in day care centers, health clinics, social service agencies, clubs, and high school graduation ceremonies.

- **Monitor how your representatives at all levels vote on key children's and family issues and hold them accountable.** Study the voting record of your U.S. senators and representatives on pages 57-78; if your state has a group that monitors state-level votes on children, get that voting record, too. Get a group to conduct the latter, if none currently exists.

If you are a public official:

- **Commit to lead and vote for the children's investment agendas** in this book.

- **Work hard to get children's issues higher on the agenda** of your elected body or your executive agencies.

- **Use your influence with candidates** to urge them to commit to a major course of action for children. Help advocate the importance of cost-saving investments in children.

- **Visit programs that serve children** in order to better understand the desperate conditions in which so many of them struggle to survive and learn.

If you are a candidate running for public office:

- **Adopt the children's investment agendas** in this book and develop additional recommendations that respond to children's needs.

- **Make a pledge to speak and vote for children.**

- **Visit programs that serve children** in order to better understand the desperate conditions in which so many of them struggle to survive and learn.

If you are a member of a community or religious organization:

Every community organization, including those that are tax-exempt and thus prohibited from participating in election activity, has a role to play in getting children's issues on the top of the nation's agenda. Your organization can:

- **Circulate public education materials** such as the State Fact Sheet on your state's performance record (order from CDF).

- **Visit editorial boards** to brief them on issues of importance to children in your state and the nation.

- **Sponsor candidate forums** on the needs of children, joining with other organizations whenever possible.

- **Organize meetings with candidates and staff** to learn more about their positions on children's issues and to provide them with information on the needs of children and how to meet them.

- **Register people to vote.**

If you are a member of the media:

- **Print or air stories on the status of children** in your community, state, and the nation; enhance your community's awareness that meeting children's needs is critical to the future of your community and the nation.

- **Question officials and candidates about where they stand on children's issues** of major concern in your state. By using your State Fact Sheet and the State Report Card you can focus on those areas in which children are doing particularly poorly, and compare your state's performance with other states.

- **Visit programs that serve children** to report on the desperate conditions in which so many of them struggle to survive and learn.

Steps CDF Will Take

IN 1990

- Through its Children 1990 campaign, seek to inject—and help others inject—children's needs and some achievable solutions to those needs into candidates', officeholders', the media's, and the public's consciousness in every state.

- Conduct campaigns to achieve a safe, affordable child care system for the children of millions of low-income working parents and to expand other critical investments in children.

- Launch a massive new SOS Black Community mobilization campaign on behalf of black children, as well as specialized campaigns on child poverty, teen pregnancy, childhood immunization, and educational achievement.

- Address public school reform issues and catalyze a range of supplemental community-based achievement and cultural enrichment models.

- Significantly increase state and local technical assistance and leadership training over the next three years. Begin a new visitation project to personalize child suffering and create a climate of urgency and action for children.

Congressional Recesses

IN 1990

During congressional recesses, you can make appointments to meet with your members of Congress in their home districts.

SENATE

February 12-19

March 12-19

April 9-17

May 25-June 4

July 2-9

August 6-September 4

HOUSE

February 9-19

April 6-17

May 25-June 4

August 6-September 4

Promises To Remember

President George Bush

Children

I think when I talk about investing in our kids, in the many proposals I've made in that area, that would be an indication of how I will pursue this objective of a "kinder and gentler" nation.

FIRST POSTELECTION PRESS CONFERENCE, NOVEMBER 9, 1988

This nation's children represent our future—and our responsibility. Good health care and nutrition, sound education, and access to safe child care should be a concern to all of us.

STATEMENT ON CHILD CARE, 1988

George Bush believes that our national character can be measured by how we care for our children—all of the nation's children—how we invest in them, how they grow, and what we convey to them.... George Bush will lead a national commitment to invest in our children.

George Bush believes our children—especially those at risk—require a more intensely focused effort by all of us....

CAMPAIGN POSITION PAPER, "INVEST IN OUR CHILDREN" OCTOBER 1988

Health

George Bush will see that quality health services so critical for improving maternal and infant health will be available to the pregnant women and young children in our nation.

George Bush will work to ensure that families have affordable public or private insurance for their children.

He will provide the leadership to focus on these needs, and will: Improve the

Reach and Effectiveness of Medicaid.... Decrease Infant Mortality.... Assure Adequate Immunization for All Children.... Provide Proper Nutrition [and].... Provide Catastrophic Protection For Very Sick and Chronically Ill Children.

"INVEST IN OUR CHILDREN," OCTOBER 1988

Child Care

The issues in child care are simple: how to provide a nurturing, safe and affordable environment....

America's working couples, America's single parents, and most importantly—America's children—deserve our attention.

STATEMENT ON CHILD CARE, 1988

The single most important issue arising from the changes in our work force is child care.... Today, child care is nothing short of a family necessity.... We must find a way to put a greater range of choices in the hands of low-income parents—because they face the greatest difficulty in meeting the demands of work and family.... Too many low-income families go without the assistance we have made available to upper income families because they do not earn enough to pay taxes....

The states and the federal government ought to provide additional resources.... for a broader range of choices and higher quality child care.

NATIONAL FEDERATION OF BUSINESS
AND PROFESSIONAL WOMEN'S CLUBS,
ALBUQUERQUE, NEW MEXICO, JULY 24, 1988

Education and Head Start

The first years of our children's lives are crucial to the success or failure of their education.... In 1970, George Bush co-sponsored the Comprehensive Head Start Child Development Act as a Congressman from Texas. He will maintain his commitment to this successful program by phasing in Head Start to reach all eligible four-year-old children.... This program works; George Bush will sharply increase its funding.

FACT SHEET ON EDUCATION, 1988

Education is our most powerful economic program, our most important trade program, and our most effective anti-poverty program. This year, the class of 2000 enters first grade. When these students graduate from high school, George Bush wants them to be the best prepared young people in the world....

The role of the federal government is to keep education on the national agenda and to target its resources to ensure access to a high quality education for those traditionally denied access, especially the disadvantaged and the disabled....

The Education President, George Bush ... will make sure that our children are offered the best education in the world.

FACT SHEET ON EDUCATION, 1988

Senate Majority Leader George Mitchell

We must meet the expectations of Americans ... for a decent future for their children.

Homelessness

We seek to halve the homeless population by the end of 1992 and to ensure access to shelter for all the needy by the end of 1995. But first, we want to get every child out of shelters and welfare hotels by the end of 1991.

Child Care

The Senate thoroughly debated and passed a bill to provide reliable, safe, and affordable child care. We could not complete final action on it this year, but it is a high priority for next year.... We must finish the child care legislation....

Education

Skilled workers will be at a premium in the coming decade. But more and more of our workers will come from schools which today are among the most disadvantaged in terms of equipment and achievement....

Early childhood education for all at-risk children by 1995 is an achievable and important goal.... it is an investment in something that we know works....

The goal of access to postsecondary education for every high school graduate by the year 2000 is ambitious. But it is realistic.

STATEMENT AT CLOSE OF FIRST SESSION
OF 101ST CONGRESS, NOVEMBER 21, 1989

The Governors in 1989

Families should not be forced to choose between care for their children and a job for themselves. We need to offer the option of extended-day programs through our schools to more of our parents.

MISSISSIPPI GOV. RAY MABUS

If we want a strong and competitive economy six years from now, we must change the education system to prepare those who today are the most neglected and least educated. If we want a state budget that is not overwhelmed by the costs of welfare and crime, then education is critical.

OHIO GOV. RICHARD F. CELESTE

The basic thrust of my priorities can be summed up in one word: children.

SOUTH CAROLINA GOV.
CARROLL A. CAMPBELL, JR.

As a nation and as a state we are losing our competitive edge. Restructuring our schools is a matter of economic survival. The world is rapidly changing and to prepare our children for the future we must educate critical thinkers who can adapt to change.

COLORADO GOV. ROY ROMER

Questions To Ask

Questions for Candidates Running for State Offices

- What will you do to improve the amount of affordable, quality child care in this state for children whose parents work outside the home? Will you support a federal initiative that makes a substantial investment in quality child care?

- What steps—through Medicaid or otherwise—would you support to provide coverage for all uninsured pregnant women and children with family incomes below twice the federal poverty level?

- Do you support including funding in our state's budget to supplement federal funds so our state can provide WIC to all the pregnant women, infants, and children in this state who need benefits?

- Will you support increases in the amount of funds that are spent to preserve families and to prevent child abuse before it occurs and before children are removed unnecessarily from their homes?

- Do you support expanded resources for schools whose children need extra assistance? How do you propose to reduce the dropout rate?

- What steps do you propose to reduce this state's high teenage pregnancy rate?

- What do you propose to reduce this states' large number of families with children that cannot find affordable housing?

- What will you do to reduce childhood poverty in this state?

Questions for Candidates Running for the U.S. House and Senate

- What child care legislation would you support to provide quality assurances and direct assistance to lower income families with child care needs? Will you support a substantial investment in quality child care?

- What will you do to improve the quality of schools serving poor children?

- What steps would you take to provide health insurance to uninsured poor and near-poor pregnant women and children?

- Do you support full federal funding for programs like Head Start, childhood immunizations, and the Special Supplemental Food Program for Women, Infants, and Children (WIC) so they can serve all children who need them?

- Do you support expanded funding for programs that help preserve families, prevent child abuse, and avoid the unnecessary removal of children from their homes?

- What will you do to help young people who graduate from high school become productively employed or gain access to higher education?

- Do you support programs to expand the supply of affordable housing for families with children, and what do you propose to do to meet the housing needs of families?

- Do you support expanded programs to treat pregnant women, mothers, and children exposed or addicted to alcohol and drugs, and what do you propose that will help prevent them from becoming dependent on drugs in the first place?

- How do you propose to reduce childhood poverty in America?

Polls To Cite

Public Support for Investment in Early Foundations for Learning

- Sixty percent of voters say that despite the federal deficit, the government should fully fund programs dealing with early childhood health and education because they save money in the long term. (Peter D. Hart Research Associates for KIDSPAC, July 1988)

Public Support for Investment in Quality Child Care for Low- and Middle-Income Families

- Sixty-one percent of those polled said the federal government should increase spending on programs to take care of the children of working parents who cannot afford care. (*Washington Post*-ABC News Poll, August 1989)

- Vast majorities of respondents in another poll agreed that both federal (72 percent) and state (74 percent) government should develop policies to make child care more available and affordable. (Child Care Action Campaign and the Great American Family Tour, "Tell the President: Your Family Matters," July 1989)

- By a two-to-one margin, child care overshadows all other needs for city children of all ages. Child care topped the list of critical needs of 91 percent of city officials responding to a survey, while half ranked lack of money as the single greatest impediment to their ability to meet this and other needs. (National League of Cities, "Our Future and Our Only Hope: A Survey of City Halls Regarding Children and Families," September 1989)

- An overwhelming 90 percent of women polled at the end of 1989 said day care was a very important issue for women today; day care ranked second behind equal pay for equal work as the most important issue. (Yankelovich Clancy Shulman for Time and CNN, October 1989)

- Seventy-five percent of all voters say the federal government should set minimum standards for health, safety, and quality of child care services. (Martilla and Kiley for American Federation of State, County and Municipal Employees and Children's Defense Fund, June 1988).

Public Support for Investment in Housing and Food for the Poor

- Three of four voters (75 percent) want federal spending on aid to the homeless increased. By nearly two to one (51 percent to 29 percent), voters would be willing to pay $100 a year or more in taxes to aid the homeless and hungry. (Millman and Lazarus Research for The National Campaign to End Hunger and Homelessness, January 1988).

Voting Record

OF 1989

Once the campaigns are over and candidates become elected officials, it is their official actions, and especially their votes, that determine whether a child has safe child care or a quality education, is immunized against preventable disease, or has access to health care.

As part of its lobbying activities, CDF monitors the positions and votes of members of Congress. To make more visible the official votes cast by members on issues and programs for children, each year CDF compiles and publishes a Nonpartisan Congressional Voting Record. CDF staff review all the floor votes and select those most critical to the lives and well-being of children, especially low-income and minority children.

For 1989 CDF has included seven votes from the Senate and eight votes from the House. Most of these votes focus on three issues that were dominant in the first session of the 101st Congress and critically important to the lives of millions of children—child care, the minimum wage, and overall national budget and spending priorities.

- Although final legislation was not completed during the first session, both the Senate and the House passed comprehensive child care bills to help low-income parents pay the cost of care and to assure all parents that child care is of decent quality.
- Most of the 12 million poor children in America live with parents who work, often at minimum wage jobs. Even full-time minimum wage employment is no longer guaranteed to ward off family poverty, however, as inflation eroded the value of the minimum wage greatly since it was last increased in 1981. Final legislation to raise the wage over two years from $3.35 per hour to $4.25 per hour and to allow a subminimum wage for teenage workers was passed and signed into law in November of 1989, after the President vetoed an earlier, better bill.
- The federal budget is a statement of the nation's priorities—determining the amount of federal funds that will be spent each year for such programs as the

military, space, agriculture, and, among many other items, children's programs. For the 1990 fiscal year, Congress developed a Budget Resolution that placed high priority on modest new spending for child and family programs for child care, health, and other critical areas.

In 1989, 33 senators and 92 representatives earned a perfect record of 100 on the CDF Voting Record. CDF applauds these lawmakers. Senators and representatives with low scores, especially scores less than 50, should be urged to take children more seriously.

CDF urges parents, child advocates, and all those concerned about children to review the key votes included in the 1989 Voting Record, to visit regularly with your representative and senators, write them, call them, and consistently inform them about the needs of children and families in your community. More votes vitally affecting children will be cast in 1990 and future years, and it is up to concerned citizens to ensure that children win each and every vote.

Members of Congress do take actions in addition to their votes that affect children in important ways. Some develop and sponsor good legislation and work tirelessly to enact it. Some members regularly speak out for children in committees and on the floor, providing the leadership that America's children so desperately need. All members cast votes in committees that have a significant impact on children, but many of those votes are cast behind closed doors and are not part of the public record.

Members may miss a crucial vote for many reasons—some unavoidable. Nevertheless, a missed vote because of an absence may affect the ultimate outcome and thus is taken into account in this rating.

The compilation of these votes was prepared by Legislate, a computerized legislative service, and is based on Legislate's record of the votes.

Senate Votes: Explanation

1. Minimum Wage (S. 4): Vote to limit increase in the minimum wage by substituting plan raising wage over three years from $3.35 per hour to $4.25 per hour along with a subminimum training wage for new hires for the plan to raise the minimum wage over three years from $3.35 per hour to $4.55 per hour with a more limited subminimum training wage. Substitute rejected 41-58 on April 11, 1989. CDF Position: **Reject.**

2. Minimum Wage (H.R. 2): Vote to raise minimum wage over three years from $3.35 per hour to $4.55 per hour with a limited training wage for inexperienced workers. Passed 62-37 on April 12, 1989. CDF Position: **Pass.**

3. FY 1990 Budget Resolution (S. Con. Res. 30): Vote to adopt Senate version of the Concurrent Budget Resolution for 1990 fiscal year, with funding allowances for new child care initiative, expansion of Medicaid for pregnant women and children, and increases in children's programs. Passed 68-31 on May 4, 1989. CDF Position: **Pass.**

4. Child Care—Tax Credit Substitute (S. 5): Vote to substitute a plan to provide tax credits to families with children for the comprehensive Act for Better Child Care legislation that would provide both tax credits and direct child care assistance. Rejected 44-56 on June 22, 1989. CDF Position. **Reject.**

5. Child Care—Act for Better Child Care (S. 5): Vote on Act for Better Child Care, as revised, combining comprehensive child care program designed to help parents pay the costs of child care and to improve the quality of care with tax credits for low-income families with children. Passed 63-37 on June 22, 1989. CDF Position: **Pass.**

6. Child Care Funding (H.R. 2990): Vote on motion to table (defeat) amendment that would delete $1.2 billion for new child care initiative from FY 1990 Labor, Health and Human Services and Education Appropriations bill. Passed 66-32 on September 21, 1989. CDF Position: **Pass.**

7. Children's Programs (H.R. 2990): Vote on annual Labor, Health and Human Services and Education Appropriations bill for FY 1990, which includes increased funding for child care, Head Start, education, child health, and child welfare programs. Passed 81-19 on September 26, 1989. CDF Position: **Pass.**

House Votes: Explanation

1. Minimum Wage (H.R. 2): Vote to limit increase in minimum wage by substituting plan raising wage from $3.35 to $4.25 over three years and instituting a six-month subminimum training wage for new employees. Rejected 198-218 on March 23, 1989. CDF Position: **Reject.**

2. Minimum Wage (H.R. 2): Vote to raise the minimum wage from $3.35 to $4.55 over three years with a two-month subminimum training wage for employees with no previous job experience. Passed 248-171 on March 23, 1989. CDF Position: **Pass.**

3. FY 1990 Budget Resolution (H. Con. Res. 106): Vote to adopt House version of the Concurrent Budget Resolution for the 1990 fiscal year, with priority funding for "Children's Initiative" including increased funds for child care, Head Start, Medicaid, and other child health and child welfare programs. Passed 263-157 on May 4, 1989. CDF Position: **Pass.**

4. Drug Wars vs. Star Wars (H.R. 2442): Vote to transfer any excess funds from the Strategic Defense Initiative (SDI) "Star Wars" program to programs under the Anti-Drug Abuse Act of 1988. Rejected 205-213 on May 24, 1989. CDF Positon: **Pass.**

5. Children's Programs (H.R. 2990): Vote on annual Labor, Health and Human Services and Education Appropriations bill for FY 1990, including increased funding for Head Start, education, and child welfare programs and reserving funds for new child care initiative. Passed 365-58 on August 2, 1989. CDF Position: **Pass.**

6. Child Care—Tax Credit Substitute (H.R. 3299): Vote on amendment that would have deleted $1.75 billion comprehensive child care provisions (H.R. 3) from omnibus Budget Reconciliation bill and substituted tax credits alone. Rejected 140-285 on October 5, 1989. CDF Position: **Reject.**

7. Child Care—Tax Credit/Title XX Substitute (H.R. 3299): Vote on amendment that would have deleted $1.75 billion comprehensive child care provisions (H.R. 3) from omnibus Budget Reconciliation bill and substituted tax credits and $200 million in Title XX funding. Rejected 195-230 on October 5, 1989. CDF Position: **Reject.**

8. FY 1990 Budget Reconciliation (H.R. 3299): Vote on motion that would have instructed House members of conference committee to delete numerous provisions from the omnibus Budget Reconciliation bill, including comprehensive child care initiative and Medicaid services for additional low-income pregnant women and children. Rejected 181-228 on October 18, 1989. CDF Position: **Reject.**

SENATE	1 Minimum Wage	2 Minimum Wage	3 Budget Resolution	4 Child Care Tax Credit Substitute	5 Child Care ABC	6 Child Care Funding	7 Children's Programs	% For (All Votes)
CDF POSITION:	N	Y	Y	N	Y	Y	Y	
ALABAMA								
HEFLIN	+	+	+	+	+	+	−	86
SHELBY	+	+	−	+	+	+	+	86
ALASKA								
MURKOWSKI	−	−	+	−	−	−	+	29
STEVENS	−	−	+	−	−	−	+	29
ARIZONA								
DECONCINI	+	+	+	+	+	+	+	100
MCCAIN	−	−	+	−	−	−	−	14
ARKANSAS								
BUMPERS	+	+	+	+	+	+	+	100
PRYOR	+	+	+	+	+	+	+	100
CALIFORNIA								
CRANSTON	+	+	+	+	+	+	+	100
WILSON	−	−	+	−	−	+	+	43
COLORADO								
ARMSTRONG	−	−	−	−	−	−	−	0
WIRTH	+	+	+	+	+	+	+	100
CONNECTICUT								
DODD	+	+	+	+	+	+	+	100
LIEBERMAN	+	+	+	+	+	+	+	100
DELAWARE								
BIDEN	+	+	+	+	+	+	+	100
ROTH	−	−	−	−	−	−	−	0
FLORIDA								
GRAHAM	+	+	+	+	+	+	+	100
MACK	−	−	+	−	−	−	+	29
GEORGIA								
FOWLER	+	+	+	+	+	+	+	100
NUNN	+	+	+	−	−	−	+	57

KEY: Y indicates CDF's position that members cast a yes vote; N indicates CDF's position that members cast a no vote; + indicates votes in support of CDF position; − indicates votes in opposition to CDF position; ? = was not present for vote; % = number of times voted for CDF position/total number of votes—absences during voting are computed as a negative vote; * indicates missed three or more votes. *Republicans in italics.*

SENATE	1 Minimum Wage	2 Minimum Wage	3 Budget Resolution	4 Child Care. Tax Credit Substitute	5 Child Care. ABC	6 Child Care Funding	7 Children's Programs	% For (All Votes)
CDF POSITION:	N	Y	Y	N	Y	Y	Y	
HAWAII								
INOUYE	+	+	+	+	+	+	+	100
MATSUNAGA	+	+	+	+	+	+	+	100
IDAHO								
MCCLURE	–	–	–	–	–	–	–	0
SYMMS	–	–	–	–	–	–	–	0
ILLINOIS								
DIXON	+	+	+	+	+	+	–	86
SIMON	+	+	+	+	+	+	+	100
INDIANA								
COATS	–	–	+	–	–	–	+	29
LUGAR	–	–	+	–	–	–	–	14
IOWA								
GRASSLEY	–	–	+	–	–	–	+	29
HARKIN	+	+	–	+	+	+	+	86
KANSAS								
DOLE	–	–	+	–	–	–	+	29
KASSEBAUM	–	–	+	–	+	+	+	57
KENTUCKY								
FORD	+	+	+	+	+	+	+	100
MCCONNELL	–	–	–	–	–	–	+	14
LOUISIANA								
BREAUX	+	+	+	+	+	–	+	86
JOHNSTON	–	+	–	+	+	+	+	71
MAINE								
COHEN	+	+	+	–	+	+	+	86
MITCHELL	+	+	+	+	+	+	+	100
MARYLAND								
MIKULSKI	+	+	+	+	+	+	+	100
SARBANES	+	+	+	+	+	+	+	100
MASSACHUSETTS								
KENNEDY	+	+	+	+	+	+	+	100
KERRY	+	+	–	+	+	+	+	86
MICHIGAN								
LEVIN	+	+	–	+	+	+	+	86
RIEGLE	+	+	+	+	+	+	+	100

SENATE	1 Minimum Wage	2 Minimum Wage	3 Budget Resolution	4 Child Care Tax Credit Substitute	5 Child Care: ABC	6 Child Care Funding	7 Children's Programs	% For (All Votes)
CDF POSITION:	N	Y	Y	N	Y	Y	Y	
MINNESOTA								
BOSCHWITZ	−	−	−	−	−	−	−	0
DURENBERGER	?	+	+	−	−	+	−	43
MISSISSIPPI								
COCHRAN	−	−	+	−	−	−	+	29
LOTT	−	−	+	−	−	−	+	29
MISSOURI								
BOND	−	−	+	−	−	+	+	43
DANFORTH	−	−	+	−	−	−	+	29
MONTANA								
BAUCUS	+	+	−	+	+	+	+	86
BURNS	−	−	+	−	−	−	+	29
NEBRASKA								
EXON	+	+	−	+	+	+	+	86
KERREY	+	+	−	+	+	+	+	86
NEVADA								
BRYAN	+	+	−	+	+	+	+	86
REID	+	+	+	+	+	+	+	100
NEW HAMPSHIRE								
HUMPHREY	−	−	−	−	−	−	−	0
RUDMAN	−	−	+	−	−	−	+	29
NEW JERSEY								
BRADLEY	+	+	+	+	+	+	+	100
LAUTENBERG	+	+	+	+	+	+	+	100
NEW MEXICO								
BINGAMAN	+	+	−	+	+	+	+	86
DOMENICI	−	−	+	−	−	?	+	29
NEW YORK								
D'AMATO	−	+	+	−	+	+	+	71
MOYNIHAN	+	+	−	+	+	+	+	86
NORTH CAROLINA								
HELMS	+	−	−	−	−	−	−	14
SANFORD	+	+	+	+	+	+	+	100
NORTH DAKOTA								
BURDICK	+	+	+	+	+	+	+	100
CONRAD	+	+	−	−	+	+	−	57

SENATE	1 Minimum Wage	2 Minimum Wage	3 Budget Resolution	4 Child Care: Tax Credit Substitute	5 Child Care: ABC	6 Child Care Funding	7 Children's Programs	% For (All Votes)
CDF POSITION:	N	Y	Y	N	Y	Y	Y	
OHIO								
GLENN	+	+	+	+	+	+	+	100
METZENBAUM	+	+	–	+	+	+	+	86
OKLAHOMA								
BOREN	–	–	–	+	+	–	+	43
NICKLES	–	–	–	–	–	–	–	0
OREGON								
HATFIELD	+	+	+	–	+	+	+	86
PACKWOOD	+	+	+	–	–	+	+	71
PENNSYLVANIA								
HEINZ	+	+	+	–	+	+	+	86
SPECTER	+	+	+	–	+	+	+	86
RHODE ISLAND								
CHAFEE	–	+	+	+	+	+	+	86
PELL	+	+	+	+	+	+	+	100
SOUTH CAROLINA								
HOLLINGS	–	–	–	+	+	+	+	57
THURMOND	–	–	+	–	–	–	+	29
SOUTH DAKOTA								
DASCHLE	+	+	+	+	+	+	+	100
PRESSLER	–	+	–	–	–	–	+	29
TENNESSEE								
GORE	+	?	+	+	+	+	+	86
SASSER	+	+	+	+	+	+	+	100
TEXAS								
BENTSEN	+	+	+	+	+	+	+	100
GRAMM	–	–	?	–	–	–	+	14
UTAH								
GARN	–	–	–	–	–	–	–	0
HATCH	–	–	+	+	+	+	–	57
VERMONT								
JEFFORDS	–	+	+	+	+	+	+	86
LEAHY	+	+	+	+	+	+	+	100
VIRGINIA								
ROBB	+	+	–	+	+	+	+	86
WARNER	–	–	–	–	–	+	–	14

SENATE	Minimum Wage 1	Minimum Wage 2	Budget Resolution 3	Child Care Tax Credit Substitute 4	Child Care ABC 5	Child Care Funding 6	Children's Programs 7	% For (All Votes)
CDF POSITION:	N	Y	Y	N	Y	Y	Y	
WASHINGTON								
ADAMS	+	+	+	+	+	+	+	100
GORTON	–	–	–	–	–	–	–	0
WEST VIRGINIA								
BYRD	+	+	+	+	+	+	+	100
ROCKEFELLER	+	+	+	+	+	+	+	100
WISCONSIN								
KASTEN	–	–	+	–	–	–	+	29
KOHL	+	+	–	+	+	+	+	86
WYOMING								
SIMPSON	–	–	+	–	–	–	+	29
WALLOP	–	–	–	–	–	?	–	0

HOUSE	1 Minimum Wage	2 Minimum Wage	3 Budget Resolution	4 Drug Wars vs. Star Wars	5 Children's Programs	6 Child Care: Tax Credit Substitute	7 Child Care: Tax Credit/ Title XX Substitute	8 Budget Reconciliation	% For (All Votes)
CDF POSITION:	N	Y	Y	Y	Y	N	N	N	
ALABAMA									
1 *CALLAHAN*	–	–	+	–	–	–	–	–	13
2 *DICKINSON*	?	–	+	–	+	–	–	–	25
3 BROWDER	0	0	+	–	+	+	–	+	67
4 BEVILL	+	+	+	–	+	+	–	+	75
5 FLIPPO	–	+	+	–	+	+	–	+	63
6 ERDREICH	+	+	+	–	+	+	–	+	75
7 HARRIS	–	+	+	–	+	+	–	+	63
ALASKA									
YOUNG, D.	–	+	+	–	+	–	–	–	38
ARIZONA									
1 *RHODES*	–	–	+	–	+	–	–	–	25
2 UDALL	+	+	+	?	+	+	+	+	88
3 *STUMP*	–	–	+	–	–	–	–	–	13
4 *KYL*	–	–	–	–	–	–	–	–	0
5 *KOLBE*	–	–	+	–	+	–	–	–	25
ARKANSAS									
1 ALEXANDER	?	+	–	+	+	+	+	+	75
2 *ROBINSON*	+	+	–	+	+	–	–	–	50
3 *HAMMERSCHMIDT*	–	–	+	–	+	–	–	–	25
4 ANTHONY	+	+	+	+	+	+	+	+	100
CALIFORNIA									
1 BOSCO	+	+	+	+	+	+	+	?	88
2 *HERGER*	–	–	–	–	–	–	–	–	0
3 MATSUI	+	+	+	+	+	+	+	+	100
4 FAZIO	+	+	+	+	+	+	+	+	100
5 PELOSI	+	+	+	+	+	+	+	?	88
6 BOXER	+	+	+	+	+	+	+	?	88
7 MILLER, G.	+	+	+	+	+	+	+	?	88
8 DELLUMS	+	+	–	+	+	+	+	?	75
9 STARK	+	+	–	+	+	+	+	?	75
10 EDWARDS, D.	+	+	+	+	+	+	+	?	88

KEY: Y indicates CDF's position that members cast a yes vote; N indicates CDF's position that members cast a no vote; + indicates votes in support of CDF position; – indicates vote in opposition to CDF position; ? = was not present for vote; 0 = not a member at time of vote; P = voted present, no position; % = number of times voted for CDF position/total number of votes—absences during voting are computed as negative votes; * indicates missed three or more votes; ** indicates Speaker of the House (votes only in a tie). *Republicans in italics.*

HOUSE	1 Minimum Wage	2 Minimum Wage	3 Budget Resolution	4 Drug Wars vs. Star Wars	5 Children's Programs	6 Child Care: Tax Credit Substitute	7 Child Care: Tax Credit/Title XX Substitute	8 Budget Reconciliation	% For (All Votes)
CDF POSITION:	N	Y	Y	Y	Y	N	N	N	
11 LANTOS	+	+	+	+	+	+	+	?	88
12 CAMPBELL, T.	–	–	+	+	+	+	–	?	50
13 MINETA	+	+	+	+	+	+	+	?	88
14 SHUMWAY	–	–	–	–	–	–	–	–	0
15 COELHO	+	+	+	+	0	0	0	0	100
15 CONDIT	0	0	0	0	0	+	+	–	67
16 PANETTA	+	+	+	–	+	+	+	?	75
17 PASHAYAN	–	+	+	–	+	?	–	–	38
18 LEHMAN, R.	+	+	+	+	+	+	+	+	100
19 LAGOMARSINO	–	–	–	–	+	–	–	–	13
20 THOMAS, WM.	–	–	+	–	+	–	–	–	25
21 GALLEGLY	–	–	+	–	–	–	–	–	13
22 MOORHEAD	–	–	–	–	–	–	–	–	0
23 BEILENSON	+	+	–	+	+	+	+	+	88
24 WAXMAN	?	?	+	+	+	+	+	+	75
25 ROYBAL	+	+	?	?	+	+	+	+	75
26 BERMAN	+	+	+	+	+	+	+	+	100
27 LEVINE, M.	+	+	–	+	+	+	+	+	88
28 DIXON	+	+	+	–	+	+	+	+	88
29 HAWKINS	+	+	+	+	+	+	+	+	100
30 MARTINEZ	?	+	+	+	+	+	+	–	75
31 DYMALLY	+	+	–	?	+	+	+	+	75
32 ANDERSON	+	+	+	+	+	+	+	+	100
33 DREIER	–	–	–	–	–	–	–	–	0
34 TORRES	+	+	+	+	?	+	+	+	88
35 LEWIS, J.	–	–	?	–	+	–	–	–	13
36 BROWN, G.	+	+	+	+	+	+	+	+	100
37 MCCANDLESS	–	–	–	–	–	–	–	–	0
38 DORNAN, R.	–	–	–	–	–	–	–	–	0
39 DANNEMEYER	–	–	–	–	–	–	–	–	0
40 COX	–	–	–	–	–	–	–	–	0
41 LOWERY, B.	–	–	+	–	+	–	–	–	25
42 ROHRABACHER	–	–	+	–	–	–	–	–	13
43 PACKARD	–	–	+	–	–	–	–	–	13
44 BATES	+	+	–	+	+	+	+	+	88
45 HUNTER	–	–	+	–	–	–	–	?	13
COLORADO									
1 SCHROEDER	+	+	–	+	+	+	+	+	88
2 SKAGGS	+	+	–	–	+	+	+	+	75
3 CAMPBELL, B	–	–	–	–	+	+	+	–	38
4 BROWN, H.	–	–	–	–	–	–	–	–	0
5 HEFLEY	–	–	–	–	–	–	–	–	0
6 SCHAEFER	–	–	–	–	–	–	–	–	0

HOUSE	1 Minimum Wage	2 Minimum Wage	3 Budget Resolution	4 Drug Wars vs. Star Wars	5 Children's Programs	6 Child Care: Tax Credit Substitute	7 Child Care: Tax Credit/Title XX Substitute	8 Budget Reconciliation	% For (All Votes)
CDF POSITION:	N	Y	Y	Y	Y	N	N	N	
CONNECTICUT									
1 KENNELLY	+	+	+	+	+	+	+	+	100
2 GEJDENSON	+	+	+	+	+	+	+	+	100
3 MORRISON, B.	+	+	−	+	+	+	+	+	88
4 *SHAYS*	+	+	−	−	+	+	+	−	63
5 *ROWLAND, JO.*	+	+	+	−	+	+	−	−	63
6 *JOHNSON, N.*	−	+	+	−	+	+	−	−	50
DELAWARE									
CARPER	+	+	−	+	+	+	+	+	88
FLORIDA									
1 HUTTO	−	−	+	−	+	−	−	−	25
2 *GRANT*	−	−	+	−	+	−	−	−	25
3 BENNETT	+	+	+	+	+	−	−	+	75
4 *JAMES*	−	−	+	−	+	−	−	−	25
5 *MCCOLLUM*	−	−	+	−	−	−	−	−	13
6 *STEARNS*	−	−	−	−	+	−	−	−	13
7 GIBBONS	+	+	+	?	+	+	+	+	88
8 *YOUNG, B.*	−	−	−	−	+	+	−	−	25
9 *BILIRAKIS*	−	−	−	−	+	−	−	−	13
10 *IRELAND*	−	−	+	−	+	−	−	−	25
11 NELSON	+	+	−	−	+	+	+	+	75
12 *LEWIS, T.*	−	−	−	−	−	−	−	−	0
13 *GOSS*	−	−	−	−	+	−	−	−	13
14 JOHNSTON, H.	+	+	+	+	+	+	+	+	100
15 *SHAW*	−	−	−	−	+	−	−	−	13
16 SMITH, L.	+	+	+	+	+	+	+	+	100
17 LEHMAN, WM.	+	+	−	+	?	+	+	?	63
18 PEPPER	?	?	?	?	0	0	0	0	0
18 *ROS–LEHTINEN*	0	0	0	0	0	−	−	−	0
19 FASCELL	+	+	+	+	+	+	+	+	100
GEORGIA									
1 THOMAS, L.	−	−	−	−	+	+	−	+	38
2 HATCHER	−	+	+	+	+	+	−	+	75
3 RAY	−	−	−	−	+	−	−	−	13
4 JONES, B.	−	+	−	+	+	+	+	+	75
5 LEWIS, J.	+	+	−	+	+	+	+	+	88
6 *GINGRICH*	−	−	+	−	+	−	−	−	25
7 DARDEN	−	+	+	−	+	+	−	+	63
8 ROWLAND, R.	−	−	+	+	+	+	−	+	63
9 JENKINS	−	+	+	+	+	+	+	?	75
10 BARNARD	−	−	+	−	+	−	−	+	38

68

HOUSE	1 Minimum Wage	2 Minimum Wage	3 Budget Resolution	4 Drug Wars vs. Star Wars	5 Children's Programs	6 Child Care: Tax Credit Substitute	7 Child Care: Tax Credit/ Title XX Substitute	8 Budget Reconciliation	% For (All Votes)
CDF POSITION:	N	Y	Y	Y	Y	N	N	N	
HAWAII									
1 *SAIKI*	–	–	+	–	+	+	+	–	50
2 AKAKA	+	+	+	+	+	+	+	+	100
IDAHO									
1 *CRAIG*	–	–	–	–	–	–	–	–	0
2 STALLINGS	–	+	+	+	+	+	–	+	75
ILLINOIS									
1 HAYES, C.	+	+	–	+	+	+	+	+	88
2 SAVAGE	?	?	–	+	+	+	+	+	63
3 RUSSO	+	+	+	+	+	+	+	+	100
4 SANGMEISTER	+	+	+	+	+	+	+	+	100
5 LIPINSKI	+	+	+	+	+	+	+	+	100
6 *HYDE*	?	?	+	–	?	–	–	–	13
7 COLLINS	+	+	–	?	?	+	+	+	63
8 ROSTENKOWSKI	+	+	+	+	+	+	+	+	100
9 YATES	+	+	–	+	+	+	+	+	88
10 *PORTER*	–	–	–	–	+	–	–	–	13
11 ANNUNZIO	+	+	+	+	+	+	+	+	100
12 *CRANE*	?	?	–	–	–	–	–	–	0
13 *FAWELL*	–	–	–	–	–	–	–	–	0
14 *HASTERT*	–	–	+	–	+	–	–	–	25
15 *MADIGAN*	–	–	+	–	+	–	–	–	25
16 *MARTIN, L.*	–	+	+	–	–	+	–	–	38
17 EVANS	+	+	+	+	+	+	+	+	100
18 *MICHEL*	–	–	?	–	+	–	–	–	13
19 BRUCE	+	+	+	+	+	+	+	+	100
20 DURBIN	+	+	+	+	+	+	+	+	100
21 COSTELLO	+	+	–	+	+	+	+	+	88
22 POSHARD	+	+	–	+	+	+	+	+	88
INDIANA									
1 VISCLOSKY	+	+	–	+	+	+	+	+	88
2 SHARP	+	+	–	+	+	+	+	+	88
3 *HILER*	–	–	+	–	+	–	–	–	25
4 LONG	0	0	–	+	+	+	+	+	83
5 JONTZ	+	+	–	+	+	+	+	+	88
6 *BURTON*	–	–	–	–	–	–	–	–	0
7 *MYERS*	–	–	+	–	+	+	–	–	38
8 MCCLOSKEY	+	+	+	+	+	+	+	+	100
9 HAMILTON	+	+	–	+	+	+	+	+	88
10 JACOBS	+	+	–	+	+	+	+	+	88

HOUSE	1 Minimum Wage	2 Minimum Wage	3 Budget Resolution	4 Drug Wars vs. Star Wars	5 Children's Programs	6 Child Care: Tax Credit Substitute	7 Child Care: Tax Credit/ Title XX Substitute	8 Budget Reconciliation	% For (All Votes)
CDF POSITION:	N	Y	Y	Y	Y	N	N	N	
IOWA									
1 *LEACH, J.*	+	+	+	−	−	+	+	−	63
2 *TAUKE*	−	−	+	−	−	−	−	+	25
3 NAGLE	+	+	−	+	+	+	+	+	88
4 SMITH, N.	+	+	−	+	+	+	+	+	88
5 *LIGHTFOOT*	−	−	−	−	−	−	−	−	0
6 *GRANDY*	−	−	+	−	+	−	−	−	25
KANSAS									
1 *ROBERTS*	−	−	−	−	−	−	−	−	0
2 SLATTERY	+	+	+	+	+	+	−	+	88
3 *MEYERS*	−	−	+	−	+	+	−	−	38
4 GLICKMAN	+	+	+	+	+	+	+	+	100
5 *WHITTAKER*	−	−	+	−	−	−	−	−	13
KENTUCKY									
1 HUBBARD	+	+	+	−	+	+	−	−	63
2 NATCHER	+	+	+	+	+	+	+	+	100
3 MAZZOLI	−	+	+	+	+	+	+	+	88
4 *BUNNING*	−	−	−	−	−	−	−	−	0
5 *ROGERS*	−	−	−	−	+	−	−	−	13
6 *HOPKINS*	−	−	−	−	+	−	−	−	13
7 PERKINS	+	+	−	+	+	+	+	+	88
LOUISIANA									
1 *LIVINGSTON*	−	−	+	−	+	−	−	−	25
2 BOGGS	+	+	+	+	+	+	+	+	100
3 TAUZIN	−	−	−	−	+	+	−	+	38
4 *MCCRERY*	−	−	+	−	+	+	−	+	38
5 HUCKABY	−	−	+	−	+	+	−	−	38
6 *BAKER*	−	−	−	−	+	−	−	−	13
7 HAYES, J.	−	+	+	+	+	+	+	?	75
8 *HOLLOWAY*	−	−	−	−	+	−	−	−	13
MAINE									
1 BRENNAN	+	+	+	+	+	+	+	+	100
2 *SNOWE*	−	−	+	−	+	+	+	−	50
MARYLAND									
1 DYSON	+	+	+	−	+	+	+	+	88
2 *BENTLEY*	−	+	−	−	+	−	−	−	25
3 CARDIN	+	+	−	+	+	+	+	+	88
4 MCMILLEN, T.	+	+	+	−	+	+	+	+	88
5 HOYER	+	+	+	+	+	+	+	+	100

HOUSE	1 Minimum Wage	2 Minimum Wage	3 Budget Resolution	4 Drug Wars vs. Star Wars	5 Children's Programs	6 Child Care: Tax Credit Substitute	7 Child Care: Tax Credit/ Title XX Substitute	8 Budget Reconciliation	% For (All Votes)
CDF POSITION:	N	Y	Y	Y	Y	N	N	N	
6 BYRON	–	–	+	–	+	+	–	+	50
7 MFUME	+	+	–	+	+	+	+	+	88
8 *MORELLA*	+	+	+	–	+	+	+	–	75
MASSACHUSETTS									
1 *CONTE*	+	+	+	–	+	+	+	+	88
2 NEAL, R.	+	+	–	+	+	+	+	+	88
3 EARLY	+	+	–	+	+	+	+	+	88
4 FRANK	+	+	–	+	+	+	+	+	88
5 ATKINS	+	+	+	+	+	+	+	+	100
6 MAVROULES	+	+	+	+	+	+	+	+	100
7 MARKEY	+	+	–	+	+	+	+	+	88
8 KENNEDY	+	+	–	+	+	+	+	+	88
9 MOAKLEY	+	+	+	+	+	+	+	+	100
10 STUDDS	+	+	–	+	+	+	+	+	88
11 DONNELLY	+	+	+	+	+	+	+	+	100
MICHIGAN									
1 CONYERS	?	+	+	+	+	+	+	+	88
2 *PURSELL*	–	–	+	–	+	–	–	–	25
3 WOLPE	+	+	+	+	+	+	+	+	100
4 *UPTON*	–	–	+	–	–	–	–	–	13
5 *HENRY*	–	–	–	–	+	–	–	–	13
6 CARR	–	+	–	+	+	+	+	–	63
7 KILDEE	+	+	+	+	+	+	+	+	100
8 TRAXLER	+	+	–	+	+	+	?	+	75
9 *VANDER JAGT*	–	–	+	–	+	–	–	–	25
10 *SCHUETTE*	–	–	–	–	+	–	–	–	13
11 *DAVIS*	+	+	+	–	+	+	+	–	75
12 BONIOR	+	+	+	+	+	+	+	+	100
13 CROCKETT	+	+	+	+	+	+	+	+	100
14 HERTEL	+	+	+	+	+	+	+	+	100
15 FORD, WM.	+	+	+	+	+	+	+	+	100
16 DINGELL	+	+	+	+	+	+	+	+	100
17 LEVIN, S.	+	+	+	+	+	+	+	+	100
18 *BROOMFIELD*	–	–	+	–	+	–	–	–	25
MINNESOTA									
1 PENNY	–	–	–	+	+	+	–	+	50
2 *WEBER*	–	–	+	–	+	–	–	–	25
3 *FRENZEL*	–	–	+	–	–	–	–	–	13
4 VENTO	+	+	+	+	+	+	+	+	100
5 SABO	+	+	–	+	+	+	+	+	88
6 SIKORSKI	+	+	–	+	+	+	+	+	88

HOUSE	1 Minimum Wage	2 Minimum Wage	3 Budget Resolution	4 Drug Wars vs. Star Wars	5 Children's Programs	6 Child Care Tax Credit Substitute	7 Child Care Tax Credit/ Title XX Substitute	8 Budget Reconciliation	% For (All Votes)
CDF POSITION:	N	Y	Y	Y	Y	N	N	N	
7 STANGELAND	–	–	+	–	+	–	–	–	25
8 OBERSTAR	+	+	+	+	+	+	+	+	100
MISSISSIPPI									
1 WHITTEN	+	+	+	–	+	+	+	+	88
2 ESPY	+	+	+	+	+	+	+	+	100
3 MONTGOMERY	–	–	+	–	+	+	–	+	50
4 PARKER	–	–	?	–	+	?	–	–	13
5 SMITH, L.	–	–	+	–	–	0	0	0	20
5 TAYLOR	0	0	0	0	0	0	0	0	0
MISSOURI									
1 CLAY	+	+	–	+	?	+	+	+	75
2 BUECHNER	–	–	+	–	+	–	–	–	25
3 GEPHARDT	+	+	+	+	+	+	+	+	100
4 SKELTON	+	+	+	–	+	+	–	+	75
5 WHEAT	+	+	–	+	+	+	+	+	88
6 COLEMAN, T.	–	–	+	–	+	–	–	–	25
7 HANCOCK	–	–	–	–	–	–	–	–	0
8 EMERSON	–	–	+	–	+	–	–	–	25
9 VOLKMER	+	+	+	+	+	+	+	+	100
MONTANA									
1 WILLIAMS	+	+	–	+	+	+	+	+	88
2 MARLENEE	–	–	?	–	+	–	–	–	13
NEBRASKA									
1 BEREUTER	–	–	–	–	+	–	–	–	13
2 HOAGLAND	+	+	–	+	+	+	+	+	88
3 SMITH, V.	–	–	?	–	+	–	–	–	13
NEVADA									
1 BILBRAY	+	+	+	+	+	+	+	+	100
2 VUCANOVICH	–	–	+	–	+	–	–	–	25
NEW HAMPSHIRE									
1 SMITH, R.	–	–	–	–	–	–	–	–	0
2 DOUGLAS	–	–	–	–	–	–	–	–	0
NEW JERSEY									
1 FLORIO	+	+	?	?	?	?	?	?	25
2 HUGHES	+	+	–	+	+	+	–	+	75
3 PALLONE	+	+	–	+	+	+	+	+	88
4 SMITH, C.	+	+	+	–	+	+	–	–	63
5 ROUKEMA	–	–	–	–	+	+	+	–	38

HOUSE	1 Minimum Wage	2 Minimum Wage	3 Budget Resolution	4 Drug Wars vs. Star Wars	5 Children's Programs	6 Child Care: Tax Credit Substitute	7 Child Care: Tax Credit/ Title XX Substitute	8 Budget Reconciliation	% For (All Votes)
CDF POSITION:	N	Y	Y	Y	Y	N	N	N	
6 DWYER	+	+	−	+	+	+	+	+	88
7 *RINALDO*	+	+	+	−	+	+	+	−	75
8 ROE	+	+	?	+	+	+	+	+	88
9 TORRICELLI	+	+	−	?	+	+	+	+	75
10 PAYNE, D.	+	+	−	+	+	+	+	+	88
11 *GALLO*	−	−	+	−	+	+	−	−	38
12 *COURTER*	?	?	−	?	+	?	?	?	13
13 *SAXTON*	−	−	−	−	+	+	−	−	25
14 GUARINI	+	+	+	+	+	+	+	+	100
NEW MEXICO									
1 *SCHIFF*	−	−	+	−	+	−	−	−	25
2 *SKEEN*	−	−	+	−	+	−	−	−	25
3 RICHARDSON	+	+	+	−	+	+	+	+	88
NEW YORK									
1 HOCHBRUECKNER	+	+	+	+	+	+	+	+	100
2 DOWNEY	+	+	+	+	+	+	+	+	100
3 MRAZEK	+	+	−	+	+	+	+	+	88
4 *LENT*	−	−	+	−	+	−	−	−	25
5 *MCGRATH*	+	−	+	+	?	+	−	−	50
6 FLAKE	+	+	+	+	+	+	+	+	100
7 ACKERMAN	+	+	+	+	+	+	+	+	100
8 SCHEUER	+	+	−	+	+	?	?	+	63
9 MANTON	+	+	+	+	+	+	+	+	100
10 SCHUMER	+	+	+	+	+	+	+	+	100
11 TOWNS	+	+	−	+	+	+	+	+	88
12 OWENS, M.	+	+	−	+	+	+	+	+	88
13 SOLARZ	+	+	+	+	+	+	+	+	100
14 *MOLINARI*	−	−	+	+	−	−	−	?	25
15 *GREEN*	−	−	+	−	+	+	−	+	50
16 RANGEL	?	+	+	+	+	+	+	+	88
17 WEISS	+	+	−	+	+	+	+	?	75
18 GARCIA	+	+	−	+	+	?	?	?	50
19 ENGEL	+	+	+	+	+	+	+	+	100
20 LOWEY, N.	+	+	−	+	+	+	+	+	88
21 *FISH*	−	−	+	−	+	+	+	−	50
22 *GILMAN*	+	+	+	−	+	+	+	−	75
23 MCNULTY	+	+	+	−	+	+	+	−	75
24 *SOLOMON*	−	−	+	−	−	−	−	−	13
25 *BOEHLERT*	+	+	+	−	+	+	+	+	88
26 *MARTIN, D.*	−	−	+	−	+	+	−	−	38
27 *WALSH*	−	+	+	−	+	−	−	−	38
28 MCHUGH	+	+	−	+	+	+	+	+	88

HOUSE	1 Minimum Wage	2 Minimum Wage	3 Budget Resolution	4 Drug Wars vs. Star Wars	5 Children's Programs	6 Child Care: Tax Credit Substitute	7 Child Care: Tax Credit/ Title XX Substitute	8 Budget Reconciliation	% For (All Votes)
CDF POSITION:	N	Y	Y	Y	Y	N	N	N	
29 *HORTON*	+	+	?	–	+	+	+	–	63
30 SLAUGHTER, L.	+	+	+	+	+	+	+	+	100
31 *PAXON*	–	–	–	–	–	–	–	–	0
32 LAFALCE	+	+	–	+	+	+	+	+	88
33 NOWAK	+	+	–	+	+	+	+	+	88
34 *HOUGHTON*	–	–	+	–	+	–	–	–	25
NORTH CAROLINA									
1 JONES, W.	+	+	+	+	+	–	+	+	88
2 VALENTINE	–	–	+	+	+	+	+	+	75
3 LANCASTER	–	–	–	+	+	+	–	+	50
4 PRICE	+	+	+	+	+	+	+	+	100
5 NEAL, S.	+	+	+	+	+	+	+	+	100
6 *COBLE*	–	–	+	–	+	–	–	–	25
7 ROSE	+	+	+	+	+	+	+	+	100
8 HEFNER	+	+	+	+	+	+	+	+	100
9 *MCMILLAN, A.*	–	–	+	–	+	+	–	–	38
10 *BALLENGER*	–	–	+	–	+	–	–	–	25
11 CLARKE	+	+	+	+	+	+	+	+	100
NORTH DAKOTA									
1 DORGAN	+	+	–	+	+	+	+	+	88
OHIO									
1 LUKEN, T.	?	?	+	+	+	+	+	+	75
2 *GRADISON*	–	–	+	?	+	–	–	–	25
3 HALL, T.	+	+	+	+	+	+	+	+	100
4 *OXLEY*	–	–	+	–	+	–	–	–	25
5 *GILLMOR*	–	–	+	–	+	+	–	–	38
6 *MCEWEN*	–	–	+	–	+	–	–	–	25
7 *DEWINE*	–	–	+	–	+	–	–	–	25
8 *LUKENS, D.*	–	–	–	?	–	–	–	–	0
9 KAPTUR	+	+	+	+	+	+	P	+	88
10 *MILLER, C.*	–	–	–	–	+	–	–	–	13
11 ECKART	+	+	+	+	+	+	+	+	100
12 *KASICH*	–	–	–	–	+	–	–	–	13
13 PEASE	+	+	–	+	+	+	+	+	88
14 SAWYER	+	+	+	+	+	+	+	+	100
15 *WYLIE*	–	?	+	–	+	–	–	–	25
16 *REGULA*	–	–	+	–	+	+	–	–	38
17 TRAFICANT	+	+	+	+	+	+	+	+	100
18 APPLEGATE	+	+	–	+	+	+	+	+	88
19 FEIGHAN	+	+	+	+	+	+	+	+	100
20 OAKAR	+	+	+	+	+	+	+	+	100
21 STOKES	+	+	+	+	+	+	+	+	100

HOUSE	1 Minimum Wage	2 Minimum Wage	3 Budget Resolution	4 Drug Wars vs. Star Wars	5 Children's Programs	6 Child Care: Tax Credit Substitute	7 Child Care: Tax Credit/ Title XX Substitute	8 Budget Reconciliation	% For (All Votes)
CDF POSITION:	N	Y	Y	Y	Y	N	N	N	
OKLAHOMA									
1 INHOFE	–	–	+	–	+	–	–	–	25
2 SYNAR	+	+	–	+	+	+	+	+	88
3 WATKINS	+	+	–	+	+	+	–	–	63
4 MCCURDY	–	+	?	–	+	+	–	+	50
5 EDWARDS, M.	–	–	+	–	+	–	–	–	25
6 ENGLISH	–	–	–	+	+	+	–	–	38
OREGON									
1 AUCOIN	+	+	+	+	+	+	+	+	100
2 SMITH, R.	–	–	+	–	+	–	–	–	25
3 WYDEN	+	+	+	+	+	+	+	+	100
4 DE FAZIO	+	+	–	+	+	+	+	+	88
5 SMITH, D.	–	?	–	–	–	–	–	–	0
PENNSYLVANIA									
1 FOGLIETTA	+	+	+	+	+	+	+	+	100
2 GRAY	+	+	+	÷	+	+	+	+	100
3 BORSKI	+	+	+	+	+	+	+	+	100
4 KOLTER	+	+	–	?	+	+	+	+	75
5 SCHULZE	–	–	?	–	+	–	–	–	13
6 YATRON	+	+	+	+	+	?	?	?	63
7 WELDON	–	–	+	–	+	+	–	–	38
8 KOSTMAYER	+	+	+	+	+	+	+	+	100
9 SHUSTER	–	–	+	–	–	–	–	–	13
10 MCDADE	+	+	+	–	+	–	–	?	63
11 KANJORSKI	+	+	–	+	+	+	+	+	88
12 MURTHA	+	+	+	–	+	+	+	+	88
13 COUGHLIN	–	–	+	–	+	+	–	–	38
14 COYNE	+	+	+	+	+	+	+	+	100
15 RITTER	–	–	–	–	+	–	–	–	13
16 WALKER	–	–	–	–	–	–	–	–	0
17 GEKAS	–	–	+	–	–	–	–	–	13
18 WALGREN	+	+	–	+	+	+	+	+	88
19 GOODLING	–	–	+	–	+	+	–	–	38
20 GAYDOS	+	+	+	–	+	+	+	+	88
21 RIDGE	+	+	+	–	+	+	–	–	63
22 MURPHY	+	+	–	+	+	+	+	+	88
23 CLINGER	–	–	+	–	+	+	–	–	38
RHODE ISLAND									
1 MACHTLEY	–	+	+	–	+	+	+	–	63
2 SCHNEIDER	+	+	+	+	+	+	+	–	88

HOUSE	1 Minimum Wage	2 Minimum Wage	3 Budget Resolution	4 Drug Wars vs. Star Wars	5 Children's Programs	6 Child Care: Tax Credit Substitute	7 Child Care: Tax Credit/ Title XX Substitute	8 Budget Reconciliation	% For (All Votes)
CDF POSITION:	N	Y	Y	Y	Y	N	N	N	
SOUTH CAROLINA									
1 *RAVENEL*	–	–	+	–	+	–	–	–	25
2 *SPENCE*	–	–	–	?	+	–	–	–	13
3 DERRICK	–	–	–	+	+	+	–	+	50
4 PATTERSON	–	–	–	–	+	+	–	+	38
5 SPRATT	–	–	–	–	+	+	+	+	50
6 TALLON	–	+	–	+	+	+	+	+	75
SOUTH DAKOTA									
1 JOHNSON, T.	+	+	–	+	+	+	+	+	88
TENNESSEE									
1 *QUILLEN*	–	–	+	–	+	–	–	–	25
2 *DUNCAN*	–	–	–	–	+	–	–	–	13
3 LLOYD	+	+	+	–	+	+	–	+	75
4 COOPER	–	+	+	–	+	+	+	+	75
5 CLEMENT	–	+	+	+	+	+	+	+	88
6 GORDON	+	+	+	+	+	+	+	+	100
7 *SUNDQUIST*	–	–	+	–	+	–	–	–	25
8 TANNER	+	+	+	+	?	+	+	+	88
9 FORD, H.	+	+	+	+	+	+	+	+	100
TEXAS									
1 CHAPMAN	–	+	+	+	+	+	+	+	88
2 WILSON	?	?	–	?	+	+	+	+	50
3 *BARTLETT*	–	–	+	–	–	–	–	–	13
4 HALL, R.	–	–	–	–	–	+	–	–	13
5 BRYANT	+	+	+	+	+	+	+	+	100
6 *BARTON*	+	–	+	–	–	–	–	–	25
7 *ARCHER*	–	–	+	–	–	–	–	–	13
8 *FIELDS*	–	–	–	–	–	–	–	–	0
9 BROOKS	+	+	+	+	+	+	+	+	100
10 PICKLE	+	+	+	+	+	+	+	+	100
11 LEATH, M.	–	–	–	–	+	+	–	+	38
12 GEREN	0	0	0	0	0	+	+	+	100
12 WRIGHT **	0	0	0	0	0	0	0	0	0
13 SARPALIUS	–	–	–	+	+	+	–	+	50
14 LAUGHLIN	–	–	+	–	+	+	+	+	63
15 DE LA GARZA	+	+	+	+	+	+	+	+	100
16 COLEMAN, R.	?	?	–	–	+	+	+	+	50
17 STENHOLM	–	–	–	+	+	–	–	+	38
18 LELAND	+	+	+	+	+	0	0	0	100
19 *COMBEST*	–	–	–	–	–	–	–	–	0
20 GONZALEZ	+	+	+	+	+	+	+	+	100

76

HOUSE	1 Minimum Wage	2 Minimum Wage	3 Budget Resolution	4 Drug Wars vs. Star Wars	5 Children's Programs	6 Child Care: Tax Credit Substitute	7 Child Care: Tax Credit/ Title XX Substitute	8 Budget Reconciliation	% For (All Votes)
CDF POSITION:	N	Y	Y	Y	Y	N	N	N	
21 *SMITH, L.*	−	−	+	−	−	−	−	−	13
22 *DELAY*	−	−	−	−	−	−	−	−	0
23 BUSTAMANTE	+	+	+	−	+	+	+	+	88
24 FROST	+	+	+	−	+	+	+	−	75
25 ANDREWS	−	+	+	−	+	+	+	+	75
26 *ARMEY*	−	−	−	−	−	−	−	−	0
27 ORTIZ	?	?	+	+	+	+	+	+	75
UTAH									
1 *HANSEN*	−	−	−	−	−	−	−	−	0
2 OWENS, W.	−	+	−	+	+	+	+	+	75
3 *NIELSON*	−	−	−	−	−	−	−	−	0
VERMONT									
1 *SMITH, P.*	−	+	+	−	+	+	+	−	63
VIRGINIA									
1 *BATEMAN*	−	−	?	−	+	−	−	−	13
2 PICKETT	−	+	+	−	+	+	+	?	63
3 *BLILEY*	−	−	+	−	+	−	−	−	25
4 SISISKY	−	+	+	−	+	+	+	+	75
5 PAYNE, L.	−	−	+	−	+	+	−	+	50
6 OLIN	+	+	−	−	+	+	+	+	75
7 *SLAUGHTER, D.*	−	−	−	−	+	−	−	−	13
8 *PARRIS*	−	−	−	?	+	−	−	−	13
9 BOUCHER	−	+	+	+	+	+	+	+	88
10 *WOLF*	−	−	+	−	+	−	−	−	25
WASHINGTON									
1 *MILLER, J.*	−	−	−	−	+	−	−	−	13
2 SWIFT	+	+	+	?	+	+	+	+	88
3 UNSOELD	+	+	+	+	+	+	+	+	100
4 *MORRISON, S.*	−	−	+	−	+	+	−	−	38
5 FOLEY**	+	+	+	+	0	0	0	0	100
6 DICKS	+	+	+	+	+	+	+	+	100
7 MCDERMOTT	+	+	+	+	+	+	+	+	100
8 *CHANDLER*	−	−	+	−	+	−	−	−	25
WEST VIRGINIA									
1 MOLLOHAN	+	+	+	−	+	+	+	+	88
2 STAGGERS	+	+	−	+	+	+	+	+	88
3 WISE	+	+	+	+	+	+	+	+	100
4 RAHALL	+	+	+	+	+	+	+	+	100

HOUSE	1 Minimum Wage	2 Minimum Wage	3 Budget Resolution	4 Drug Wars vs. Star Wars	5 Children's Programs	6 Child Care: Tax Credit Substitute	7 Child Care: Tax Credit/ Title XX Substitute	8 Budget Reconciliation	% For (All Votes)
CDF POSITION:	N	Y	Y	Y	Y	N	N	N	
WISCONSIN									
1 ASPIN	+	+	+	–	+	+	+	+	88
2 KASTENMEIER	+	+	–	+	+	+	+	+	88
3 *GUNDERSON*	–	–	+	–	+	–	–	–	25
4 KLECZKA	+	+	+	+	+	+	+	+	100
5 MOODY	+	+	–	+	+	+	+	+	88
6 *PETRI*	–	–	+	–	+	–	–	–	25
7 OBEY	+	+	–	+	+	+	+	+	88
8 *ROTH*	–	–	–	–	–	–	–	–	0
9 *SENSENBRENNER*	–	–	?	–	–	–	–	–	0
WYOMING									
1 *CHENEY*	0	0	0	0	0	0	0	0	0
1 *THOMAS, C.*	0	0	+	–	+	–	–	–	33

Part V: Appendix

HOW STATE PERFORMANCE FOR
CHILDREN WAS MEASURED

•

STATE PERFORMANCE TABLES

•

TECHNICAL NOTES

HOW STATE

Performance for Children

WAS MEASURED

To build the State Report Card, CDF selected 20 measures of performance for children. Ten measures evaluate the adequacy of each state's progress in improving children's status and 10 evaluate the adequacy of state investment in programs of proven effectiveness for children. For each of the 20 measures, CDF set a threshold for adequacy, which was used to award or withhold credit to states. The definitions of adequacy for each performance measure are stated at the top of each table that follows.

Each measure for which the state met or exceeded the threshold counts for five points. Thus, states' total scores can range from 0 to 100 percent. For example, a state that received credit on 15 measures would score 75 percent (15 "yes" measures times five points per measure).

The 20 measures were selected because each is a strong indicator of the status of children or of the adequacy of state investment in programs of proven effectiveness for children. Not included are many critical indicators of children's well-being and state performance that could not be presented for all states, because neither the federal nor state governments collect the necessary data. For example, we cannot provide information on how many children in each state are at risk of abuse or neglect. Nor can we show on a state-by-state basis how many children are not adequately immunized or suffer from a preventable disability.

However, the indicators we have chosen are substantial measures of the health and well-being of children. They are measured consistently and collected regularly by the federal government and the states. The Technical Notes contain more detailed information on data sources and calculations made for each measure.

Measurement of Children's Well-Being

The first set of 10 measures examines state performance in improving children's well-being over the past decade. The indicators shown in Tables 1 through 10 measure progress over a period of at least five years, in order to ensure that the trends we have identified are reliable. However, not all of the measures cover the

81

same time period, because the official reporting systems from which they come vary substantially in the timing and the amount of information they yield. Sources of data and any calculations made by the Children's Defense Fund are noted in the Technical Notes.

For each measure in this set, the tables provide several pieces of information for each state:

- **The first two columns** for each state show: a measure for the first year of the time period that is being measured; and the state's rank compared with all other states in that first year.
- **The second two columns** show the measure in question for the last year of the time period examined; and the state's rank compared with other states in the last year.
- **The third two columns** show the state's progress (or lack of progress) over the time period in question; and how the state's *rate of progress* compared with all other states during the time period in question.
- **The last column** indicates whether the state's rate of progress meets the definition of adequate progress. States are not simply given credit because they are making progress (that is, improving children's status). They also must improve at a certain *rate of progress.*

Definitions of Adequate Progress: Because these 10 indicators look at adequacy of progress *over time,* states are rewarded for their rate of progress rather than their most recent status. In other words, a state with relatively low rank on measures nonetheless could receive a relatively high score if the state is making sufficient progress. Similarly, a state that ranks relatively high in the most recent year would rank poorly if the status of its children either had declined or failed to improve sufficiently.

For the three health measures, the thresholds for adequate progress are based on goals for 1990 established by the U.S. Surgeon General. For measures that are not addressed by an official goal set by the federal government or a national organization, credit generally is awarded for progress made at a rate greater than or equal to the national rate of progress. The exception is the child poverty indicator; child poverty is such a fundamental measure of children's well-being that we awarded credit only if the state reduced its child poverty rate.

Measurement of State Investments in Children

The second set of measures evaluates state performance in making adequate investments in children's programs of proven effectiveness in saving lives and money or improving health. In other words, how hard is each state trying to prevent or ameliorate the problems faced by children?

For this set of measures, state performance is evaluated based on information about states' programs or policies for children in the most recent year available published in special surveys or government studies; sources of data and any calculations made by the Children's Defense Fund are noted in the Technical Notes.

The columns in this set of measures (Tables 11-20) are explained in the table itself or in the Technical Notes. In each chart, however, the *last column* indicates whether the state meets the definition of adequate investment in children's programs.

Definitions of Adequate Investment: For some program measures, the definition of adequacy was whether the state had taken advantage of *all* major federally allowed options. For example, states received credit if they extend Medicaid eligibility to all pregnant women and infants with family incomes up to 185 percent of the federal poverty level; if the state set an income threshold lower than this, it would not receive credit.

For other programs, the definition of adequacy was any allocation of state revenues to supplement federal funding so that additional numbers of eligible children could benefit from programs that have proven their effectiveness. For example, states that supplement Head Start or WIC received credit.

For a few programs, definitions of adequacy were based on standards set by national professional organizations. For instance, we used recommended staff ratios for infants in day care set by the National Association for the Education of Young Children, and students-per-teacher ratios that have been recommended by professional education groups such as the National Association of Elementary School Principals and the National Education Association.

For programs in which none of these independent standards or goals were available, the definition of adequacy became whether state performance in the most recent year exceeded the national average. For example, in the absence of performance targets for state child support enforcement efforts, states received credit for scoring at least as high as the national average in collecting child support amounts owed.

TABLE 1
Early Prenatal Care

Definition of Adequate Progress: Based on recent rates of change, will the state achieve the U.S. Surgeon General's 1990 goal of ensuring that 90 percent of all infants are born to pregnant women who begin prenatal care in the first three months of pregnancy?

	Percent of All Live Births With Early Prenatal Care				1978-1987 Change		Is State's Progress Adequate?
	1978	Rank	1987	Rank	Percent	Rank	
United States Total	74.9%	—	76.0%	—	1.5%	—	Yes 0/No 50 (Not Available 1)
Alabama	71.2	39	73.6	39	3.4	24	No
Alaska	71.6	37	76.4	31	6.7	6	No
Arizona	66.6	48	70.1	45	5.3	14	No
Arkansas	68.5	47	68.6	47	.1	37	No
California	73.2	33	75.9	32	3.7	22	No
Colorado	76.7	21	77.4	26	.9	31	No
Connecticut	86.3	3	85.7	1	-.7	40	No
Delaware	75.2	25	77.7	24	3.3	25	No
District of Columbia	58.1	50	60.5	50	4.1	19	No
Florida	69.8	42	69.4	46	-.6	39	No
Georgia	71.5	38	72.4	42	1.3	30	No
Hawaii	72.0	36	76.8	29	6.7	6	No
Idaho	74.2	30	74.9	36	.9	31	No
Illinois	74.2	30	78.5	22	5.8	12	No
Indiana	77.3	19	77.9	23	.8	33	No
Iowa	83.6	4	85.4	2	2.2	28	No
Kansas	78.9	11	80.7	14	2.3	27	No
Kentucky	69.6	43	75.9	32	9.1	1	No
Louisiana	75.1	27	75.4	35	.4	35	No
Maine	78.6	14	83.5	4	6.2	8	No
Maryland	81.2	7	80.5	15	-.9	42	No
Massachusetts	87.8	1	83.3	6	-5.1	48	No
Michigan	76.9	20	80.8	13	5.1	15	No
Minnesota	76.0	24	80.4	17	5.8	12	No
Mississippi	72.1	35	76.5	30	6.1	9	No
Missouri	75.2	25	80.3	18	6.8	5	No
Montana	78.4	15	77.2	27	-1.5	43	No
Nebraska	77.7	17	82.4	8	6.0	11	No
Nevada	74.7	28	73.2	40	-2.0	46	No
New Hampshire	80.5	9	83.4	5	3.6	23	No
New Jersey	77.4	18	80.5	15	4.0	20	No
New Mexico	n/a	n/a	56.4	51	n/a	n/a	n/a
New York	69.1	45	71.4	43	3.3	25	No
North Carolina	74.4	29	77.6	25	4.3	17	No
North Dakota	76.7	21	82.1	10	7.0	4	No
Ohio	78.8	12	81.9	11	3.9	21	No
Oklahoma	68.8	46	73.0	41	6.1	9	No
Oregon	74.2	30	73.7	38	-.7	40	No
Pennsylvania	79.8	10	78.6	21	-1.5	43	No
Rhode Island	87.3	2	83.8	3	-4.0	47	No
South Carolina	70.4	41	66.3	49	-5.8	50	No
South Dakota	69.3	44	74.3	37	7.2	3	No
Tennessee	72.4	34	75.8	34	4.7	16	No
Texas	70.9	40	67.3	48	-5.1	48	No
Utah	81.7	6	82.2	9	.6	34	No
Vermont	78.7	13	79.0	20	.4	35	No
Virginia	81.0	8	80.9	12	-.1	38	No
Washington	78.4	15	77.1	28	-1.7	45	No
West Virginia	65.1	49	70.3	44	8.0	2	No
Wisconsin	82.1	5	83.3	6	1.5	29	No
Wyoming	76.1	23	79.4	19	4.3	17	No

TABLE 2
Infant Mortality

Definition of Adequate Progress: Based on recent rates of change, will the state achieve the U.S. Surgeon General's 1990 goal of reducing the infant mortality rate to nine or fewer deaths per 1,000 live births?

	Infant Deaths Per 1,000 Live Births				1978-1987 Change		Is State's Progress Adequate?
	1978	Rank	1987	Rank	Percent	Rank	
United States Total	13.8	—	10.1	—	−26.8%	—	Yes 30/No 21
Alabama	16.1	45	12.2	47	−24.2	29	No
Alaska	14.4	38	10.4	34	−27.8	18	No
Arizona	13.1	22	9.5	20	−27.5	21	Yes
Arkansas	16.4	46	10.3	33	−37.2	4	Yes
California	11.8	11	9.0	14	−23.7	33	Yes
Colorado	11.2	5	9.8	26	−12.5	49	No
Connecticut	11.6	8	8.8	11	−24.1	30	Yes
Delaware	13.2	24	11.7	43	−11.4	50	No
District of Columbia	27.3	51	19.3	51	−29.3	15	No
Florida	14.1	34	10.6	38	−24.8	28	No
Georgia	15.4	43	12.7	48	−17.5	47	No
Hawaii	11.1	3	8.9	13	−19.8	45	Yes
Idaho	11.7	10	10.4	34	−11.1	51	No
Illinois	15.7	44	11.6	42	−26.1	25	No
Indiana	13.1	22	10.1	30	−22.9	38	No
Iowa	12.6	16	9.1	15	−27.8	18	Yes
Kansas	12.5	13	9.5	20	−24.0	32	Yes
Kentucky	12.7	17	9.7	24	−23.6	34	Yes
Louisiana	17.3	48	11.8	45	−31.8	11	No
Maine	10.4	1	8.3	4	−20.2	44	Yes
Maryland	14.7	39	11.5	41	−21.8	42	No
Massachusetts	11.1	3	7.2	1	−35.1	7	Yes
Michigan	13.8	31	10.7	39	−22.5	40	No
Minnesota	12.0	12	8.7	9	−27.5	21	Yes
Mississippi	18.7	50	13.7	50	−26.7	23	No
Missouri	14.8	40	10.2	31	−31.1	13	Yes
Montana	11.6	8	10.0	29	−13.8	48	No
Nebraska	13.0	19	8.6	7	−33.8	9	Yes
Nevada	12.5	13	9.6	22	−23.2	36	Yes
New Hampshire	10.4	1	7.8	2	−25.0	27	Yes
New Jersey	13.0	19	9.4	19	−27.7	20	Yes
New Mexico	14.1	34	8.1	3	−42.6	1	Yes
New York	14.0	33	10.7	39	−23.6	34	No
North Carolina	16.6	47	11.9	46	−28.3	17	No
North Dakota	13.5	26	8.7	9	−35.6	6	Yes
Ohio	13.3	25	9.3	18	−30.1	14	Yes
Oklahoma	14.3	36	9.6	22	−32.9	10	Yes
Oregon	12.9	18	10.4	34	−19.4	46	No
Pennsylvania	13.7	30	10.4	34	−24.1	30	No
Rhode Island	13.6	28	8.4	5	−38.2	2	Yes
South Carolina	18.6	49	12.7	48	−31.7	12	No
South Dakota	13.5	26	9.9	28	−26.7	23	Yes
Tennessee	14.8	40	11.7	43	−20.9	43	No
Texas	14.3	36	9.1	15	−36.4	5	Yes
Utah	11.4	7	8.8	11	−22.8	39	Yes
Vermont	13.6	28	8.5	6	−37.5	3	Yes
Virginia	13.8	31	10.2	31	−26.1	25	Yes
Washington	12.5	13	9.7	24	−22.4	41	Yes
West Virginia	15.1	42	9.8	26	−35.1	7	Yes
Wisconsin	11.2	5	8.6	7	−23.2	36	Yes
Wyoming	13.0	19	9.2	17	−29.2	16	Yes

85

TABLE 3
Low–Birthweight Births

Definition of Adequate Progress: Based on recent rates of change, will the state achieve the U.S. Surgeon General's 1990 goal of reducing the proportion of infants born at low birthweight to no more than 5 percent of all births?

	Proportion of Low-Birthweight Infants				1978-1987 Change		Is State's Progress Adequate?
	1978	Rank	1987	Rank	Percent	Rank	
United States Total	7.1%	—	6.9%	—	−2.8%	—	Yes 5/No 46
Alabama	8.4	45	8.0	45	−4.8	20	No
Alaska	5.3	3	4.8	1	−9.4	5	Yes
Arizona	6.1	15	6.4	19	4.9	50	No
Arkansas	7.9	41	7.7	39	−2.5	27	No
California	6.4	18	6.0	17	−6.3	11	No
Colorado	8.2	44	7.9	43	−3.7	23	No
Connecticut	6.7	22	6.7	23	.0	34	No
Delaware	7.2	29	6.7	23	−6.9	7	No
District of Columbia	13.1	51	13.5	51	3.1	48	No
Florida	7.8	38	7.7	39	−1.3	31	No
Georgia	8.7	47	8.2	47	−5.7	13	No
Hawaii	7.2	29	7.0	31	−2.8	26	No
Idaho	5.6	8	5.6	14	.0	34	No
Illinois	7.4	33	7.4	37	.0	34	No
Indiana	6.5	20	6.5	21	.0	34	No
Iowa	5.3	3	5.1	5	−3.8	22	No
Kansas	6.3	17	6.4	19	1.6	46	No
Kentucky	7.1	27	6.8	26	−4.2	21	No
Louisiana	8.9	49	8.7	49	−2.2	29	No
Maine	5.4	6	5.4	9	.0	34	No
Maryland	7.8	38	7.8	42	.0	34	No
Massachusetts	6.5	20	5.7	15	−12.3	4	No
Michigan	7.2	29	7.2	36	.0	34	No
Minnesota	5.3	3	5.0	4	−5.7	13	Yes
Mississippi	8.8	48	9.0	50	2.3	47	No
Missouri	7.0	25	7.0	31	.0	34	No
Montana	5.6	8	5.5	12	−1.8	30	No
Nebraska	5.8	14	5.5	12	−5.2	19	No
Nevada	7.4	33	6.9	27	−6.8	8	No
New Hampshire	5.6	8	4.9	2	−12.5	3	Yes
New Jersey	7.5	36	7.0	31	−6.7	10	No
New Mexico	8.6	46	7.1	34	−17.4	1	No
New York	7.7	37	7.6	38	−1.3	31	No
North Carolina	8.1	42	7.9	43	−2.5	27	No
North Dakota	5.4	6	4.9	2	−9.3	6	Yes
Ohio	7.0	25	6.6	22	−5.7	13	No
Oklahoma	7.1	27	6.7	23	−5.6	16	No
Oregon	5.1	1	5.4	9	5.9	51	No
Pennsylvania	6.9	24	6.9	27	.0	34	No
Rhode Island	6.4	18	6.0	17	−6.3	11	No
South Carolina	8.9	49	8.6	48	−3.4	25	No
South Dakota	5.2	2	5.2	6	.0	34	No
Tennessee	8.1	42	8.1	46	.0	34	No
Texas	7.3	32	6.9	27	−5.5	17	No
Utah	5.7	13	5.7	15	.0	34	No
Vermont	6.2	16	5.3	7	−14.5	2	Yes
Virginia	7.4	33	6.9	27	−6.8	8	No
Washington	5.6	8	5.3	7	−5.4	18	No
West Virginia	6.8	23	7.1	34	4.4	49	No
Wisconsin	5.6	8	5.4	9	−3.6	24	No
Wyoming	7.8	38	7.7	39	−1.3	31	No

TABLE 4
Teen Birth Rate

Definition of Adequate Progress: Has the state achieved a reduction in the number of teens giving birth (per 1,000 females ages 15–19) greater than the national rate of reduction?

	Births to Females Ages 15-19 Per 1,000 Women of those Ages				1980-1986 Change		Is State's Progress Adequate?
	1980	Rank	1986	Rank	Percent	Rank	
United States Total	53.0	—	50.6	—	-4.5%	—	Yes 34/No 16 (Not Available 1)
Alabama	68.3	42	61.8	42	-9.5	21	Yes
Alaska	64.4	37	52.3	32	-18.8	6	Yes
Arizona	65.5	40	68.0	45	3.8	46	No
Arkansas	74.5	47	69.1	46	-7.2	28	Yes
California	53.3	26	54.9	35	3.0	45	No
Colorado	49.9	20	47.1	24	-5.6	30	Yes
Connecticut	30.5	2	31.2	4	2.3	44	No
Delaware	51.2	23	49.8	27	-2.7	37	No
District of Columbia	62.4	35	n/a	n/a	n/a	n/a	n/a
Florida	58.5	32	57.7	37	-1.4	42	No
Georgia	71.9	44	65.8	44	-8.5	25	Yes
Hawaii	50.7	21	45.6	22	-10.1	20	Yes
Idaho	59.5	34	44.0	18	-26.1	2	Yes
Illinois	55.8	27	49.7	26	-10.9	19	Yes
Indiana	57.5	29	50.1	28	-12.9	15	Yes
Iowa	43.0	12	33.0	5	-23.3	3	Yes
Kansas	56.8	28	51.4	31	-9.5	21	Yes
Kentucky	72.3	45	61.1	40	-15.5	10	Yes
Louisiana	76.0	49	69.5	47	-8.6	24	Yes
Maine	47.4	17	41.5	14	-12.4	17	Yes
Maryland	43.4	13	45.5	21	4.8	47	No
Massachusetts	28.1	1	30.2	2	7.5	49	No
Michigan	45.0	14	44.0	18	-2.2	40	No
Minnesota	35.4	7	30.1	1	-15.0	11	Yes
Mississippi	83.7	51	73.7	50	-11.9	18	Yes
Missouri	57.8	31	53.2	34	-8.0	26	Yes
Montana	48.5	19	42.4	15	-12.6	16	Yes
Nebraska	45.1	15	36.8	9	-18.4	7	Yes
Nevada	58.5	32	58.4	38	-.2	43	No
New Hampshire	33.6	4	30.5	3	-9.2	23	Yes
New Jersey	35.2	6	34.2	7	-2.8	36	No
New Mexico	71.8	43	69.9	48	-2.6	38	No
New York	34.8	5	37.0	11	6.3	48	No
North Carolina	57.5	29	56.0	36	-2.6	38	No
North Dakota	41.7	11	34.3	8	-17.7	9	Yes
Ohio	52.5	24	49.2	25	-6.3	29	Yes
Oklahoma	74.6	48	64.8	43	-13.1	14	Yes
Oregon	50.9	22	43.4	17	-14.7	12	Yes
Pennsylvania	40.5	10	39.9	13	-1.5	41	No
Rhode Island	33.0	3	36.8	9	11.5	50	No
South Carolina	64.8	38	61.4	41	-5.2	33	Yes
South Dakota	52.6	25	43.0	16	-18.3	8	Yes
Tennessee	64.1	36	59.3	39	-7.5	27	Yes
Texas	74.3	46	70.4	49	-5.2	33	Yes
Utah	65.2	39	50.4	29	-22.7	4	Yes
Vermont	39.5	8	33.8	6	-14.4	13	Yes
Virginia	48.3	18	45.7	23	-5.4	32	Yes
Washington	46.7	16	44.1	20	-5.6	30	Yes
West Virginia	67.8	41	52.5	33	-22.6	5	Yes
Wisconsin	39.5	8	37.8	12	-4.3	35	No
Wyoming	78.7	50	50.8	30	-35.5	1	Yes

TABLE 5
Births to Unmarried Women

Definition of Adequate Progress: Has the state experienced a smaller increase in the percent of births that were to unmarried women than has the nation as a whole?

	Percent of Births That Were to Unmarried Mothers				1980-1987 Change		Is State's Progress Adequate?
	1980	Rank	1987	Rank	Percent	Rank	
United States Total	18.4%	—	24.5%	—	33.2%	—	Yes 22/No 29
Alabama	22.2	41	26.8	38	20.7	7	Yes
Alaska	15.6	24	22.0	26	41.0	30	No
Arizona	18.7	34	27.2	39	45.5	38	No
Arkansas	20.5	38	24.6	33	20.0	6	Yes
California	21.4	40	27.2	39	27.1	17	Yes
Colorado	13.0	11	18.9	12	45.4	37	No
Connecticut	17.9	33	23.5	30	31.3	19	Yes
Delaware	24.2	48	27.7	42	14.5	3	Yes
District of Columbia	56.5	51	59.7	51	5.7	1	Yes
Florida	23.0	43	27.5	41	19.6	5	Yes
Georgia	23.2	45	28.0	43	20.7	7	Yes
Hawaii	17.6	29	21.3	24	21.0	9	Yes
Idaho	7.9	2	13.0	2	64.6	48	No
Illinois	22.5	42	28.1	44	24.9	12	Yes
Indiana	15.5	23	22.0	26	41.9	31	No
Iowa	10.3	5	16.2	6	57.3	46	No
Kansas	12.3	9	17.2	10	39.8	28	No
Kentucky	15.1	22	20.7	18	37.1	26	No
Louisiana	23.4	46	31.9	49	36.3	25	No
Maine	13.9	18	19.8	16	42.4	32	No
Maryland	25.2	49	31.5	48	25.0	13	Yes
Massachusetts	15.7	25	20.9	22	33.1	22	Yes
Michigan	16.2	28	20.4	17	25.9	15	Yes
Minnesota	11.4	7	17.1	9	50.0	41	No
Mississippi	28.0	50	35.1	50	25.4	14	Yes
Missouri	17.6	29	23.7	32	34.7	24	No
Montana	12.5	10	19.4	14	55.2	45	No
Nebraska	11.6	8	16.8	8	44.8	35	No
Nevada	13.5	15	16.4	7	21.5	10	Yes
New Hampshire	11.0	6	14.7	4	33.6	23	No
New Jersey	21.1	39	23.5	30	11.4	2	Yes
New Mexico	16.1	27	29.6	46	83.9	50	No
New York	23.8	47	29.7	47	24.8	11	Yes
North Carolina	19.0	35	24.9	34	31.1	18	Yes
North Dakota	9.2	4	13.9	3	51.1	42	No
Ohio	17.8	32	24.9	34	39.9	29	No
Oklahoma	14.0	20	20.7	18	47.9	39	No
Oregon	14.8	21	22.4	28	51.4	43	No
Pennsylvania	17.7	31	25.3	36	42.9	33	No
Rhode Island	15.7	25	21.8	25	38.9	27	No
South Carolina	23.0	43	29.0	45	26.1	16	Yes
South Dakota	13.4	14	19.4	14	44.8	35	No
Tennessee	19.9	37	26.3	37	32.2	21	Yes
Texas	13.3	13	19.0	13	42.9	33	No
Utah	6.2	1	11.1	1	79.0	49	No
Vermont	13.7	17	18.0	11	31.4	20	Yes
Virginia	19.2	36	22.8	29	18.8	4	Yes
Washington	13.6	16	20.8	21	52.9	44	No
West Virginia	13.1	12	21.1	23	61.1	47	No
Wisconsin	13.9	18	20.7	18	48.9	40	No
Wyoming	8.2	3	15.8	5	92.7	51	No

TABLE 6
Paternities Established

Definition of Adequate Progress: Has the state increased the number of paternities established per 1,000 births to unmarried women at a rate greater than the national average?

	Paternities Established Per 1,000 Births to Unmarried Women				1981-1987 Change		Is State's Progress Adequate?
	1981	Rank	1987	Rank	Percent	Rank	
United States Total	237.7	—	273.0	—	14.9%	—	Yes 23/No 27 (Not Available 1)
Alabama	352.3	9	438.6	9	24.5	22	Yes
Alaska	44.2	50	142.0	38	221.3	4	Yes
Arizona	57.2	45	58.6	47	2.4	31	No
Arkansas	89.9	42	626.7	5	597.1	1	Yes
California	249.5	18	205.3	31	-17.7	41	No
Colorado	157.2	30	126.9	40	-19.3	42	No
Connecticut	489.7	3	353.8	16	-27.8	44	No
Delaware	311.8	12	680.9	3	118.4	10	Yes
District of Columbia	172.8	29	167.5	37	-3.1	35	No
Florida	229.4	23	264.7	24	15.4	23	Yes
Georgia	252.5	16	492.6	8	95.1	14	Yes
Hawaii	241.6	21	267.4	23	10.7	25	No
Idaho	47.7	48	185.2	34	288.3	2	Yes
Illinois	142.1	33	411.4	12	189.5	6	Yes
Indiana	92.0	41	206.8	30	124.8	9	Yes
Iowa	277.4	15	270.7	22	-2.4	34	No
Kansas	223.7	24	168.7	36	-24.6	43	No
Kentucky	245.1	19	364.1	15	48.6	17	Yes
Louisiana	148.1	31	124.0	42	-16.3	39	No
Maine	143.2	32	284.9	20	99.0	13	Yes
Maryland	638.0	1	291.7	19	-54.3	48	No
Massachusetts	300.1	13	398.8	13	32.9	21	Yes
Michigan	465.1	4	636.2	4	36.8	19	Yes
Minnesota	315.4	11	346.9	17	10.0	26	No
Mississippi	129.3	36	126.9	40	-1.9	33	No
Missouri	34.6	51	n/a	n/a	n/a	n/a	n/a
Montana	50.7	46	75.2	45	48.3	18	Yes
Nebraska	82.0	43	177.2	35	116.1	11	Yes
Nevada	185.3	27	193.8	33	4.6	28	No
New Hampshire	45.9	49	77.7	44	69.3	15	Yes
New Jersey	553.0	2	523.1	7	-5.4	37	No
New Mexico	233.7	22	51.1	49	-78.1	50	No
New York	202.4	26	227.9	28	12.6	24	No
North Carolina	414.7	6	426.3	11	2.8	30	No
North Dakota	291.0	14	793.6	1	172.7	8	Yes
Ohio	250.6	17	232.8	27	-7.1	38	No
Oklahoma	92.4	39	51.8	48	-43.9	46	No
Oregon	343.3	10	219.3	29	-36.1	45	No
Pennsylvania	243.8	20	368.6	14	51.2	16	Yes
Rhode Island	179.9	28	196.1	32	9.0	27	No
South Carolina	124.9	37	260.5	25	108.6	12	Yes
South Dakota	78.6	44	248.1	26	215.6	5	Yes
Tennessee	414.6	7	428.3	10	3.3	29	No
Texas	47.9	47	11.9	50	-75.2	49	No
Utah	396.9	8	328.8	18	-17.2	40	No
Vermont	220.9	25	747.8	2	238.5	3	Yes
Virginia	129.8	35	129.7	39	-.1	32	No
Washington	97.2	38	277.9	21	185.9	7	Yes
West Virginia	129.9	34	61.0	46	-53.0	47	No
Wisconsin	439.8	5	595.3	6	35.4	20	Yes
Wyoming	92.4	39	88.3	43	-4.4	36	No

TABLE 7
Children in Poverty

Definition of Adequate Progress: Has the state achieved any reduction in the percentage of children living in poverty?

	Percent of Children Under 18 Who Are Poor				1979-1985 Change		Is State's Progress Adequate?
	1979	Rank	1985	Rank	Percent	Rank	
United States Total	16.0%	—	20.9%	—	30.6%	—	Yes 2/No 49
Alabama	23.6	49	31.7	50	34.3	33	No
Alaska	12.1	14	12.7	3	5.0	7	No
Arizona	16.5	35	21.2	32	28.5	28	No
Arkansas	23.4	47	29.0	46	23.9	23	No
California	15.2	31	21.4	35	40.8	35	No
Colorado	11.5	9	16.2	16	40.9	36	No
Connecticut	11.4	7	11.8	2	3.5	5	No
Delaware	15.6	32	15.3	10	−1.9	2	Yes
District of Columbia	27.0	50	31.3	49	15.9	19	No
Florida	18.5	37	21.1	31	14.1	15	No
Georgia	21.1	44	24.2	43	14.7	16	No
Hawaii	13.0	17	16.7	19	28.5	28	No
Idaho	14.3	26	21.7	36	51.7	40	No
Illinois	14.9	29	22.8	38	53.0	43	No
Indiana	11.9	12	18.4	23	54.6	46	No
Iowa	11.5	9	21.3	33	85.2	50	No
Kansas	11.4	7	14.5	7	27.2	27	No
Kentucky	21.6	45	23.6	41	9.3	11	No
Louisiana	23.5	48	30.6	48	30.2	30	No
Maine	15.8	34	16.0	14	1.3	4	No
Maryland	12.5	16	13.0	4	4.0	6	No
Massachusetts	13.1	18	14.1	6	7.6	10	No
Michigan	13.3	20	22.7	37	70.7	49	No
Minnesota	10.2	4	16.3	17	59.8	47	No
Mississippi	30.4	51	34.3	51	12.8	14	No
Missouri	14.6	28	20.5	29	40.4	34	No
Montana	13.8	22	20.1	27	45.7	37	No
Nebraska	12.1	14	18.7	25	54.5	45	No
Nevada	10.0	3	15.2	9	52.0	42	No
New Hampshire	9.4	2	6.2	1	−34.0	1	Yes
New Jersey	14.1	25	15.5	11	9.9	12	No
New Mexico	22.1	46	27.5	45	24.4	25	No
New York	19.0	40	23.6	41	24.2	24	No
North Carolina	18.3	36	19.5	26	6.6	9	No
North Dakota	14.3	26	16.4	18	14.7	16	No
Ohio	13.2	19	20.2	28	53.0	43	No
Oklahoma	15.7	33	21.0	30	33.8	32	No
Oregon	12.0	13	17.7	22	47.5	39	No
Pennsylvania	13.9	23	18.4	23	32.4	31	No
Rhode Island	13.6	21	16.7	19	22.8	21	No
South Carolina	21.0	43	23.5	40	11.9	13	No
South Dakota	20.0	41	21.3	33	6.5	8	No
Tennessee	20.6	42	25.2	44	22.3	20	No
Texas	18.7	39	23.3	39	24.6	26	No
Utah	10.7	6	13.2	5	23.4	22	No
Vermont	13.9	23	16.1	15	15.8	18	No
Virginia	14.9	29	14.9	8	.0	3	No
Washington	11.5	9	16.9	21	47.0	38	No
West Virginia	18.5	37	30.4	47	64.3	48	No
Wisconsin	10.4	5	15.8	13	51.9	41	No
Wyoming	7.7	1	15.5	11	101.3	51	No

TABLE 8
Affordability of Housing for the Poor

Definition of Affordable: In 1989, was the fair market rental (FMR) price for a two–bedroom apartment in the state's metropolitan region with the lowest such rent 30 percent or less of the 1989 federal poverty line income for a family of four, as recommended by the federal government?

	Two-Bedroom FMR Price as a Percent of Poverty for a Family of 4				1979-1989 Change		Is State's Housing Affordable for the Poor?
	1979	Rank	1989	Rank	Percent	Rank	
United States Total	—	—	—	—	—	—	Yes 1/No 50
Alabama	27.5	1	30.2	1	9.8%	19	Yes
Alaska	76.9	50	52.7	44	−31.5	1	No
Arizona	42.3	43	52.6	43	24.3	39	No
Arkansas	30.0	5	34.4	12	14.7	26	No
California	39.5	38	40.5	28	2.5	15	No
Colorado	36.1	29	43.5	33	20.5	34	No
Connecticut	38.5	37	45.1	35	17.1	30	No
Delaware	47.8	46	54.3	45	13.6	25	No
District of Columbia	49.4	47	67.0	51	35.6	46	No
Florida	36.6	31	33.0	5	−9.8	3	No
Georgia	31.4	10	33.6	8	7.0	18	No
Hawaii	63.8	49	62.5	50	−2.0	8	No
Idaho	41.6	42	50.7	41	21.9	37	No
Illinois	36.9	32	41.6	31	12.7	24	No
Indiana	32.5	16	34.2	11	5.2	17	No
Iowa	32.4	13	40.4	26	24.7	41	No
Kansas	37.2	35	40.9	29	9.9	20	No
Kentucky	32.5	16	33.0	5	1.5	13	No
Louisiana	29.3	3	35.4	17	20.8	35	No
Maine	36.9	32	44.6	34	20.9	36	No
Maryland	46.5	44	35.9	18	−22.8	2	No
Massachusetts	35.8	27	50.1	40	39.9	47	No
Michigan	32.7	18	46.5	39	42.2	48	No
Minnesota	40.5	39	41.1	30	1.5	13	No
Mississippi	35.9	28	35.3	16	−1.7	9	No
Missouri	30.8	8	31.6	2	2.6	16	No
Montana	35.5	24	42.1	32	18.6	31	No
Nebraska	32.4	13	40.4	26	24.7	41	No
Nevada	49.4	47	59.4	49	20.2	33	No
New Hampshire	46.6	45	57.4	47	23.2	38	No
New Jersey	34.0	21	45.5	36	33.8	45	No
New Mexico	35.0	23	38.8	23	10.9	23	No
New York	33.0	20	57.1	46	73.0	50	No
North Carolina	32.7	18	33.1	7	1.2	12	No
North Dakota	40.5	39	40.0	24	−1.2	10	No
Ohio	31.4	10	34.8	14	10.8	21	No
Oklahoma	30.3	7	34.8	14	14.9	28	No
Oregon	38.2	36	45.7	37	19.6	32	No
Pennsylvania	27.8	2	36.1	20	29.9	44	No
Rhode Island	41.1	41	51.1	42	24.3	39	No
South Carolina	34.6	22	32.8	4	−5.2	4	No
South Dakota	32.4	13	37.5	21	15.7	29	No
Tennessee	35.6	25	34.0	9	−4.5	5	No
Texas	30.0	5	34.4	12	14.7	26	No
Utah	36.1	29	40.0	24	10.8	21	No
Vermont	n/a	n/a	58.4	48	n/a	n/a	No
Virginia	35.6	25	34.0	9	−4.5	5	No
Washington	31.9	12	32.1	3	.6	11	No
West Virginia	37.1	34	35.9	18	−3.2	7	No
Wisconsin	29.6	4	37.9	22	28.0	43	No
Wyoming	30.9	9	46.4	38	50.2	49	No

TABLE 9
High School Graduation

Definition of Adequate Progress: Has the state increased its graduation rate (the percentage of ninth–graders finishing high school four years later) by an amount greater than the national average?

	Percent of 9th Graders Who Graduate Four Years Later				1982-1987 Change		Is State's Progress Adequate?
	1982	Rank	1987	Rank	Percent	Rank	
United States Total	69.5%	—	71.1%	—	2.3%	—	Yes 29/No 22
Alabama	63.4	44	70.2	34	10.7	7	Yes
Alaska	64.3	41	66.7	41	3.7	19	Yes
Arizona	63.4	44	64.4	45	1.6	32	No
Arkansas	73.4	23	77.5	18	5.6	15	Yes
California	60.1	49	66.1	42	10.0	8	Yes
Colorado	70.9	29	73.7	26	3.9	18	Yes
Connecticut	70.6	31	80.5	11	14.0	3	Yes
Delaware	68.2	34	70.1	35	2.8	22	Yes
District of Columbia	56.9	50	55.5	51	-2.5	44	No
Florida	60.2	48	58.6	50	-2.7	45	No
Georgia	65.0	39	62.5	47	-3.8	47	No
Hawaii	74.9	18	70.8	33	-5.5	49	No
Idaho	74.4	20	78.8	14	5.9	12	Yes
Illinois	76.1	14	75.7	22	-.5	41	No
Indiana	71.7	27	73.7	26	2.8	22	Yes
Iowa	84.1	2	86.4	5	2.7	25	Yes
Kansas	80.7	7	82.1	9	1.7	31	No
Kentucky	65.9	38	67.4	39	2.3	29	Yes
Louisiana	52.9	51	60.1	49	13.6	4	Yes
Maine	70.1	32	79.3	13	13.1	5	Yes
Maryland	74.8	19	74.5	23	-.4	40	No
Massachusetts	76.4	13	76.5	20	.1	38	No
Michigan	71.6	28	62.4	48	-12.8	51	No
Minnesota	88.2	1	90.6	1	2.7	25	Yes
Mississippi	61.3	47	64.8	44	5.7	14	Yes
Missouri	74.2	21	74.4	24	.3	36	No
Montana	78.7	9	86.2	6	9.5	9	Yes
Nebraska	81.9	6	86.7	4	5.9	12	Yes
Nevada	64.8	40	72.1	31	11.3	6	Yes
New Hampshire	77.0	11	72.7	29	-5.6	50	No
New Jersey	76.5	12	77.2	19	.9	34	No
New Mexico	69.4	33	71.7	32	3.3	21	Yes
New York	63.4	44	62.9	46	-.8	42	No
North Carolina	67.1	36	67.8	37	1.0	33	No
North Dakota	83.9	3	88.4	3	5.4	16	Yes
Ohio	77.5	10	82.8	8	6.8	11	Yes
Oklahoma	70.8	30	72.6	30	2.5	27	Yes
Oregon	72.4	25	72.8	28	.6	35	No
Pennsylvania	76.0	16	78.7	15	3.6	20	Yes
Rhode Island	72.7	24	69.4	36	-4.5	48	No
South Carolina	63.8	42	66.9	40	4.9	17	Yes
South Dakota	82.7	5	79.7	12	-3.6	46	No
Tennessee	67.8	35	67.8	37	.0	39	No
Texas	63.6	43	65.1	43	2.4	28	Yes
Utah	75.0	17	80.6	10	7.5	10	Yes
Vermont	79.6	8	78.0	16	-2.0	43	No
Virginia	73.8	22	74.0	25	.3	36	No
Washington	76.1	14	77.8	17	2.2	30	No
West Virginia	66.3	37	76.2	21	14.9	2	Yes
Wisconsin	83.1	4	85.4	7	2.8	22	Yes
Wyoming	72.4	25	89.3	2	23.3	1	Yes

TABLE 10
Youth Unemployment

Definition of Adequate Progress: Has the state reduced the percentage of unemployed youths, ages 16–19, by more than the national rate of reduction?

	Percent of Youths Ages 16-19 Who Are Unemployed				1982-1988 Change		Is State's Progress Adequate?
	1982	Rank	1988	Rank	Percent	Rank	
United States Total	23.2%	—	15.3%	–	−34.1%	—	Yes 25/No 26
Alabama	31.6	48	17.6	39	−44.3	18	Yes
Alaska	17.5	11	17.9	40	2.3	46	No
Arizona	25.2	38	17.4	37	−31.0	29	No
Arkansas	29.1	46	21.0	46	−27.8	32	No
California	23.4	30	15.7	33	−32.9	28	No
Colorado	18.6	14	18.4	41	−1.1	44	No
Connecticut	18.3	12	5.5	1	−69.9	1	Yes
Delaware	24.9	36	10.0	6	−59.8	5	Yes
District of Columbia	36.9	51	20.0	43	−45.8	17	Yes
Florida	22.6	25	14.0	26	−38.1	24	Yes
Georgia	21.2	18	18.5	42	−12.7	38	No
Hawaii	22.3	22	10.7	11	−52.0	10	Yes
Idaho	18.4	13	15.3	30	−16.8	35	No
Illinois	23.3	28	16.3	34	−30.0	30	No
Indiana	24.8	35	12.0	15	−51.6	11	Yes
Iowa	17.4	9	15.2	29	−12.6	39	No
Kansas	11.6	1	13.0	19	12.1	50	No
Kentucky	27.6	43	20.6	45	−25.4	33	No
Louisiana	27.6	43	28.9	51	4.7	47	No
Maine	22.8	26	10.6	10	−53.5	9	Yes
Maryland	23.6	31	15.6	31	−33.9	26	No
Massachusetts	21.4	19	9.7	4	−54.7	7	Yes
Michigan	28.7	45	17.5	38	−39.0	22	Yes
Minnesota	14.3	6	10.2	8	−28.7	31	No
Mississippi	31.1	47	27.4	50	−11.9	40	No
Missouri	21.7	21	20.0	43	−7.8	43	No
Montana	19.8	16	16.8	36	−15.2	37	No
Nebraska	16.2	7	13.4	22	−17.3	34	No
Nevada	22.8	26	13.3	21	−41.7	20	Yes
New Hampshire	16.2	7	10.0	6	−38.3	23	Yes
New Jersey	22.5	24	10.4	9	−53.8	8	Yes
New Mexico	24.2	33	24.5	48	1.2	45	No
New York	22.3	22	11.8	14	−47.1	14	Yes
North Carolina	23.6	31	12.4	17	−47.5	13	Yes
North Dakota	13.1	4	11.7	13	−10.7	41	No
Ohio	27.5	42	15.6	31	−43.3	19	Yes
Oklahoma	13.1	4	14.8	27	13.0	51	No
Oregon	25.6	39	13.6	23	−46.9	15	Yes
Pennsylvania	23.3	28	13.9	25	−40.3	21	Yes
Rhode Island	27.0	41	9.7	4	−64.1	4	Yes
South Carolina	24.4	34	13.1	20	−46.3	16	Yes
South Dakota	12.0	2	11.0	12	−8.3	42	No
Tennessee	34.3	50	14.8	27	−56.9	6	Yes
Texas	20.4	17	21.8	47	6.9	49	No
Utah	19.0	15	12.2	16	−35.8	25	Yes
Vermont	17.4	9	5.5	1	−68.4	3	Yes
Virginia	25.8	40	12.9	18	−50.0	12	Yes
Washington	25.1	37	16.6	35	−33.9	26	No
West Virginia	32.0	49	26.8	49	−16.3	36	No
Wisconsin	21.6	20	6.5	3	−69.9	1	Yes
Wyoming	13.0	3	13.8	24	6.2	48	No

TABLE 11
Medicaid Coverage of Babies and Pregnant Women

Definition of Adequate State Investment: By the end of 1989, did the state provide Medicaid coverage to all pregnant women and infants (up to age one) with incomes below 185 percent of the federal poverty level?

	State Income Eligibility Level (as a percent of poverty)	Is State's Investment Adequate?
United States Total	—	Yes 15/No 36
Alabama	100%	No
Alaska	100%	No
Arizona	100%	No
Arkansas	100%	No
California	185%	Yes
Colorado	75%	No
Connecticut	185%	Yes
Delaware	100%	No
District of Columbia	100%	No
Florida	150%	No
Georgia	100%	No
Hawaii	185%	Yes
Idaho	75%	No
Illinois	100%	No
Indiana	100%	No
Iowa	185%	Yes
Kansas	150%	No
Kentucky	125%	No
Louisiana	100%	No
Maine	185%	Yes
Maryland	185%	Yes
Massachusetts	185%	Yes
Michigan	185%	Yes
Minnesota	185%	Yes
Mississippi	185%	Yes
Missouri	100%	No
Montana	100%	No
Nebraska	100%	No
Nevada	75%	No
New Hampshire	75%	No
New Jersey	100%	No
New Mexico	100%	No
New York	185%	Yes
North Carolina	150%	No
North Dakota	75%	No
Ohio	100%	No
Oklahoma	100%	No
Oregon	85%	No
Pennsylvania	100%	No
Rhode Island	185%	Yes
South Carolina	185%	Yes
South Dakota	100%	No
Tennessee	100%	No
Texas	130%	No
Utah	100%	No
Vermont	185%	Yes
Virginia	100%	No
Washington	185%	Yes
West Virginia	150%	No
Wisconsin	120%	No
Wyoming	100%	No

TABLE 12
Medicaid Coverage of Poor Children

Definition of Adequate State Investment: By October 1989, did the state provide Medicaid coverage to all children younger than six and living in families with incomes below 100 percent of the federal poverty level?

	Maximum Age of Poor Children Covered by 10/89	Is State's Investment Adequate?
United States Total	—	Yes 17/No 34
Alabama	1	No
Alaska	2	No
Arizona	6	Yes
Arkansas	6	Yes
California	*	Yes
Colorado	18*	No
Connecticut	1	No
Delaware	3	No
District of Columbia	3	No
Florida	6	Yes
Georgia	3	No
Hawaii	5	No
Idaho	*	No
Illinois	1	No
Indiana	3	No
Iowa	6	Yes
Kansas	5	No
Kentucky	2	No
Louisiana	6	Yes
Maine	6	Yes
Maryland	2	No
Massachusetts	5	No
Michigan	3	No
Minnesota	6	Yes
Mississippi	5	No
Missouri	3	No
Montana	1	No
Nebraska	3	No
Nevada	6	Yes
New Hampshire	*	No
New Jersey	2	No
New Mexico	3	No
New York	1	No
North Carolina	6	Yes
North Dakota	*	No
Ohio	1	No
Oklahoma	2	No
Oregon	3	No
Pennsylvania	3	No
Rhode Island	6	Yes
South Carolina	6	Yes
South Dakota	2	No
Tennessee	6	Yes
Texas	4	No
Utah	1	No
Vermont	6	Yes
Virginia	2	No
Washington	6	Yes
West Virginia	6	Yes
Wisconsin	1	No
Wyoming	6	Yes

*See Technical Notes

TABLE 13
Nutritional Assistance for Mothers and Children

Definition of Adequate State Investment: Does the state supplement federal WIC funds (the Special Supplemental Food Program for Women, Infants, and Children) to provide food *and* nutrition services to additional women and children?

	Est. Number of Eligible Women and Children, in 1984*	Number of WIC Parti- cipants*, August 1989	Percent of Eligible Population Served	Is State's Investment Adequate?*
United States Total	7,307,580	4,357,546	59.6%	Yes 10/No 41
Alabama	172,345	94,203	54.7	No
Alaska	14,888	9,192	61.7	Yes
Arizona	109,554	64,786	62.1	No
Arkansas	109,166	54,104	49.6	No
California	778,857	458,379	59.2	No
Colorado	84,750	47,423	66.5	No
Connecticut	64,360	49,208	76.5	No
Delaware	18,305	10,440	57.0	Yes
District of Columbia	19,036	12,478	83.5	Yes
Florida	299,461	172,435	57.6	No
Georgia	229,471	165,120	72.0	No
Hawaii	38,892	13,780	35.4	No
Idaho	52,249	21,390	40.9	No
Illinois	319,732	189,010	61.0	Yes
Indiana	167,976	94,766	56.4	No
Iowa	85,359	45,288	54.0	No
Kansas	75,609	40,187	55.0	No
Kentucky	153,900	87,386	58.0	No
Louisiana	188,736	113,093	68.4	No
Maine	43,267	17,191	39.7	No
Maryland	98,209	47,545	48.4	No
Massachusetts	132,164	74,429	56.3	Yes
Michigan	256,550	143,213	65.8	No
Minnesota	107,351	70,885	67.3	Yes
Mississippi	143,400	100,491	70.1	No
Missouri	157,275	83,321	53.0	No
Montana	31,208	13,866	44.4	No
Nebraska	51,765	21,662	46.5	No
Nevada	21,038	15,830	75.2	No
New Hampshire	24,514	13,222	57.6	No
New Jersey	173,250	88,174	50.9	No
New Mexico	68,241	33,170	52.7	No
New York	558,005	369,135	66.7	Yes
North Carolina	216,919	132,913	61.4	No
North Dakota	25,388	16,492	65.0	No
Ohio	313,828	181,267	57.8	No
Oklahoma	115,205	56,335	48.9	No
Oregon	80,379	49,142	61.6	No
Pennsylvania	307,322	208,598	67.9	Yes
Rhode Island	24,910	14,747	59.2	No
South Carolina	133,738	87,013	65.1	No
South Dakota	33,960	17,594	53.5	No
Tennessee	175,147	96,811	60.8	No
Texas	580,213	342,387	59.0	Yes
Utah	91,702	44,567	48.6	No
Vermont	18,507	14,819	80.1	No
Virginia	158,595	88,534	55.8	No
Washington	119,679	54,436	45.5	No
West Virginia	69,930	30,332	43.4	No
Wisconsin	122,602	76,933	62.8	Yes
Wyoming	13,141	9,824	74.8	No

* See Technical Notes

TABLE 14
Support for Early Childhood Education

Definition of Adequate State Investment: Does the state provide state revenues either to supplement federal Head Start funds or for its own state preschool education program?

	1985 Head Start En-rollments per 100 Poor Children, Ages 3-5	Rank	1988 Head Start Supplement	1988 State-Funded Preschool	Is State's Investment Adequate?
United States Total	15.5	—	Yes 9/No 42	Yes 26/No 25	Yes 29/No 22
Alabama	15.7	26	No	No	No
Alaska	19.5	10	Yes	Yes	Yes
Arizona	9.9	50	No	No	No
Arkansas	16.0	24	No	No	No
California	11.7	43	No	Yes	Yes
Colorado	18.7	13	No	No	No
Connecticut	25.3	4	Yes	No	Yes
Delaware	18.6	15	No	Yes	Yes
District of Columbia	27.6	2	No	Yes	Yes
Florida	11.6	44	No	Yes	Yes
Georgia	14.8	31	No	No	No
Hawaii	15.6	27	Yes	No	Yes
Idaho	10.5	49	No	No	No
Illinois	15.5	28	No	Yes	Yes
Indiana	13.7	34	No	No	No
Iowa	11.1	47	No	No	No
Kansas	17.9	18	No	No	No
Kentucky	22.5	6	No	Yes	Yes
Louisiana	13.9	33	No	Yes	Yes
Maine	18.2	16	Yes	Yes	Yes
Maryland	20.1	7	No	Yes	Yes
Massachusetts	19.7	8	Yes	Yes	Yes
Michigan	18.2	16	No	Yes	Yes
Minnesota	13.4	36	Yes	Yes	Yes
Mississippi	55.8	1	No	No	No
Missouri	16.8	21	No	Yes	Yes
Montana	12.6	40	No	No	No
Nebraska	12.2	41	No	No	No
Nevada	7.5	51	No	No	No
New Hampshire	26.8	3	No	No	No
New Jersey	17.4	19	No	Yes	Yes
New Mexico	16.7	22	No	No	No
New York	12.1	42	No	Yes	Yes
North Carolina	18.7	13	No	No	No
North Dakota	11.3	46	No	No	No
Ohio	19.2	11	Yes*	Yes	Yes
Oklahoma	19.7	8	No	Yes	Yes
Oregon	12.7	39	No	Yes	Yes
Pennsylvania	16.0	24	No	Yes	Yes
Rhode Island	18.8	12	Yes	No	Yes
South Carolina	16.1	23	No	Yes	Yes
South Dakota	13.1	37	No	No	No
Tennessee	15.4	29	No	No	No
Texas	10.7	48	No	Yes	Yes
Utah	13.1	37	No	No	No
Vermont	23.1	5	No	Yes	Yes
Virginia	14.5	32	No	No	No
Washington	11.5	45	Yes	Yes	Yes
West Virginia	13.7	34	No	Yes	Yes
Wisconsin	17.2	20	No	Yes	Yes
Wyoming	15.2	30	No	No	No

*See Technical Notes

TABLE 15
Child Care Quality: Staff Ratio

Definition of Adequate State Effort: As of 1989, did the state limit the maximum number of infants (at age nine months) per staff person in licensed child care centers to no more than four infants for every child care worker, as recommended by the National Association for the Education of Young Children?

	Maximum Number of Infants Per Child Care Worker	Is State's Effort Adequate?
National Median	4*	Yes 30/No 20 (Not Applicable 1)
Alabama	6	No
Alaska	5	No
Arizona	5	No
Arkansas	6	No
California	4	Yes
Colorado	5	No
Connecticut	4	Yes
District of Columbia	4	Yes
Delaware	7	No
Florida	6	No
Georgia	7	No
Hawaii	n/a*	n/a
Idaho	12	No
Illinois	4	Yes
Indiana	4	Yes
Iowa	4	Yes
Kansas	3	Yes
Kentucky	6	No
Louisiana	6	No
Maine	4	Yes
Maryland	3	Yes
Massachusetts	3	Yes
Michigan	4	Yes
Minnesota	4	Yes
Mississippi	5	No
Missouri	4	Yes
Montana	4	Yes
Nebraska	4	Yes
Nevada	4*	Yes
New Hampshire	4	Yes
New Jersey	4	Yes
New Mexico	6	No
New York	4	Yes
North Carolina	7	No
North Dakota	4	Yes
Ohio	6	No
Oklahoma	4	Yes
Oregon	4	Yes
Pennsylvania	4	Yes
Rhode Island	4	Yes
South Carolina	8	No
South Dakota	5	No
Tennessee	5*	No
Texas	5	No
Utah	4	Yes
Vermont	4	Yes
Virginia	4	Yes
Washington	4	Yes
West Virginia	4	Yes
Wisconsin	4	Yes
Wyoming	5	No

*See Technical Notes

TABLE 16
State Child Support Collection Efforts

Definition of Adequate State Effort: In 1988 did the state collect child support amounts due from obligated parents at a rate equal to or above the national average?

	Total Child Support Enforcement Caseload	Total Child Support Obligations Due	Total Child Support Obligations Paid*	Percent of Amount Due Paid	Is State's Effort Adequate?
United States Total	11,068,147	$18,431,679,279	$4,278,076,984	23.4%	Yes 19/No 30/Not Available 2
Alabama	228,549	143,958,126	48,340,418	33.5	Yes
Alaska	28,253	140,185,751	23,794,098	16.9	No
Arizona	134,253	74,935,365	26,674,266	35.5	Yes
Arkansas	65,463	104,189,137	21,269,751	20.4	No
California	930,855	2,121,140,077	431,132,572	20.3	No
Colorado	196,074	228,547,089	35,130,642	15.3	No
Connecticut	100,695	110,719,333	65,706,754	59.3	Yes
Delaware	23,561	61,230,000	18,404,000	30.0	Yes
District of Columbia	63,305	52,081,073	8,798,854	16.8	No
Florida	513,007	714,915,333	137,371,556	19.2	No
Georgia	330,820	405,591,414	72,639,792	17.9	No
Hawaii	51,666	94,637,000	19,095,000	20.1	No
Idaho	36,751	116,486,330	17,827,828	15.3	No
Illinois	505,063	264,416,636	110,348,950	41.7	Yes
Indiana	301,324	n/a	n/a	n/a	n/a
Iowa	90,223	228,235,505	31,188,929	13.6	No
Kansas	91,259	219,808,670	29,924,221	13.6	No
Kentucky	192,888	328,917,009	41,859,801	12.7	No
Louisiana	182,427	153,368,506	50,845,873	33.1	Yes
Maine	51,300	192,082,970	34,488,799	17.9	No
Maryland	196,664	821,835,340	221,848,903	26.9	Yes
Massachusetts	216,792	663,964,568	155,395,186	23.4	Yes
Michigan	886,531	2,800,593,072	551,342,921	19.6	No
Minnesota	142,573	315,436,060	115,116,672	36.4	Yes
Mississippi	193,855	153,001,920	20,390,614	13.3	No
Missouri	179,739	523,688,145	58,934,012	11.2	No
Montana	21,644	74,973,175	6,141,069	8.1	No
Nebraska	57,031	332,441,741	49,865,973	14.9	No
Nevada	33,924	110,235,860	17,978,114	16.3	No
New Hampshire	20,768	92,063,138	21,032,550	22.8	No
New Jersey	351,429	1,103,131,328	285,852,114	25.9	Yes
New Mexico	68,524	57,378,013	10,690,630	18.6	No
New York	722,159	899,078,662	292,609,801	32.5	Yes
North Carolina	229,863	310,831,738	89,230,399	28.7	Yes
North Dakota	20,808	16,021,885	6,476,610	40.4	Yes
Ohio	653,776	471,480,556	94,882,436	20.1	No
Oklahoma	172,207	149,878,000	20,906,281	13.9	No
Oregon	181,034	412,576,148	66,963,363	16.2	No
Pennsylvania	763,160	992,008,360	529,228,875	53.3	Yes
Rhode Island	39,467	30,785,185	15,904,945	51.6	Yes
South Carolina	135,051	46,634,643	21,079,734	45.2	Yes
South Dakota	18,172	57,918,412	9,158,546	15.8	No
Tennessee	291,149	178,309,539	57,725,539	32.3	Yes
Texas	345,935	819,719,986	89,075,639	10.8	No
Utah	51,554	224,394,082	48,265,383	21.5	No
Vermont	15,399	28,361,759	7,085,227	24.9	Yes
Virginia	198,792	288,834,666	90,611,377	31.3	Yes
Washington	217,277	559,315,300	81,912,501	14.6	No
West Virginia	87,451	68,068,646	12,969,933	19.0	No
Wisconsin	256,859	n/a	n/a	n/a	n/a
Wyoming	17,415	73,274,019	4,559,533	6.2	No

* See Technical Notes

TABLE 17
Change in AFDC Benefits Compared With Inflation

Definition of Adequate State Investment: Between 1970 and 1989, did the state increase the maximum AFDC payment for a family of three at a rate that kept pace with inflation*?

| | AFDC Maximum Benefit for a Three-Person Family | | | | 1970-89 Change | | |
| | July 1970 | | January 1989 | | | | |
	Monthly Amount	Percent of Poverty	Monthly Amount	Percent of Poverty	(in real $) Percent	Rank	Is State's Investment Adequate?
U. S. (Median State)	$184	71%	$360	46%	−37%	—	Yes 2/No 49
Alabama	65	25	118	15	−42	38	No
Alaska	328	127	809	83	−21	8	No
Arizona	138	53	293	37	−32	24	No
Arkansas	89	34	204	26	−26	15	No
California	186	72	663	84	15	1	Yes
Colorado	193	75	356	45	−41	36	No
Connecticut	283	110	623	79	−29	18	No
Delaware	160	62	333	42	−33	26	No
District of Columbia	195	76	293	50	−35	28	No
Florida	114	44	387	37	−19	6	No
Georgia	107	41	270	34	−19	6	No
Hawaii	226	88	557	62	−21	8	No
Idaho	211	82	304	39	−54	48	No
Illinois	232	90	342	44	−53	47	No
Indiana	120	47	288	37	−23	11	No
Iowa	201	78	394	50	−37	31	No
Kansas	222	86	427	54	−38	32	No
Kentucky	147	57	218	28	−52	46	No
Louisiana	88	34	190	24	−31	20	No
Maine	135	52	438	56	4	2	Yes
Maryland	162	63	377	48	−25	13	No
Massachusetts	268	104	539	69	−35	28	No
Michigan (Wayne Co.)*	219	85	513	65	−25	13	No
Minnesota	256	99	532	68	−33	26	No
Mississippi	56	22	120	15	−31	20	No
Missouri	104	40	285	36	−12	4	No
Montana	202	78	359	46	−43	40	No
Nebraska	171	66	364	46	−32	24	No
Nevada	121	47	330	42	−12	4	No
New Hampshire	262	102	496	63	−39	34	No
New Jersey	302	117	424	54	−55	49	No
New Mexico	149	58	264	34	−43	40	No
New York (NYC)*	279	108	539	69	−38	32	No
North Carolina	145	56	266	34	−41	36	No
North Dakota	213	83	386	49	−42	38	No
Ohio	161	62	321	41	−36	30	No
Oklahoma	152	59	325	41	−31	20	No
Oregon	184	71	420	53	−27	16	No
Pennsylvania	265	103	402	51	−51	45	No
Rhode Island	229	89	517	66	−27	16	No
South Carolina	85	33	206	26	−22	10	No
South Dakota	264	102	366	47	−55	49	No
Tennessee	112	43	173	22	−50	44	No
Texas	148	57	184	23	−60	51	No
Utah	175	68	376	48	−31	20	No
Vermont	267	103	629	80	−24	12	No
Virginia	225	87	354	45	−49	43	No
Washington	258	100	492	63	−39	34	No
West Virginia	114	44	249	32	−30	19	No
Wisconsin	184	71	517	66	−10	3	No
Wyoming	213	83	360	46	−46	42	No

* See Technical Notes

100

TABLE 18
Adequacy of AFDC Benefits in Relation to Housing Costs

Definition of Adequate State Investment: Does the state's AFDC maximum benefit level for a family of three allow them to rent housing for no more than 30 percent of the family's monthly income, as recommended by the federal government?

	2-Bedroom HUD Fair Market Rent* (October 1989)	3-Person Family Maximum AFDC Grant (January 1989)	HUD Fair Market Rent's Percent of AFDC Grant	Is State's Investment Adequate?
United States Total	—	$360 (median state)	—	Yes 0/No 51
Alabama	$313	118	265%	No
Alaska	547	809	68	No
Arizona	546	293	186	No
Arkansas	357	204	175	No
California	420	663	63	No
Colorado	451	356	127	No
Conneticut	468	623	75	No
Delaware	565	333	170	No
District of Columbia	695	293	237	No
Florida	342	387	88	No
Georgia	349	270	129	No
Hawaii	649	557	117	No
Idaho	526	304	173	No
Illinois	432	342	126	No
Indiana	355	288	123	No
Iowa	419	394	106	No
Kansas	424	427	99	No
Kentucky	342	218	157	No
Louisiana	367	190	193	No
Maine	463	438	106	No
Maryland	373	377	99	No
Massachusetts	520	539	96	No
Mich (Wayne Co)*	483	513	94	No
Minnesota	427	532	80	No
Mississippi	366	120	305	No
Missouri	328	285	115	No
Montana	437	359	122	No
Nebraska	419	364	115	No
Nevada	616	330	187	No
New Hampshire	596	496	120	No
New Jersey	472	424	111	No
New Mexico	403	264	153	No
New York (NYC)*	593	539	110	No
North Carolina	344	266	129	No
North Dakota	415	386	108	No
Ohio	361	321	112	No
Oklahoma	361	325	111	No
Oregon	474	420	113	No
Pennsylvania	375	402	93	No
Rhode Island	530	517	103	No
South Carolina	340	206	165	No
South Dakota	389	366	106	No
Tennessee	353	173	204	No
Texas	357	184	194	No
Utah	415	376	110	No
Vermont	606	629	96	No
Virginia	353	354	100	No
Washington	333	492	68	No
West Virginia	373	249	150	No
Wisconsin	393	517	76	No
Wyoming	482	360	134	No

* See Technical Notes

TABLE 19
Students-Per-Teacher Ratio

Definition of Adequate State Effort: Does the state's public school students-per-teacher ratio (in 1988) fall at or below 15:1, as recommended by professional education organizations?

	1982 Student-per-Teacher		1988 Student-per-Teacher		1982-88 Change		Is State's Effort Adequate?
	Ratio	Rank	Ratio	Rank	Percent	Rank	
United States Total	18.9	—	17.6	—	−6.9	—	Yes 8/No 43
Alabama	20.7	43	19.3	43	−6.8	25	No
Alaska	16.0	9	17.3	29	8.1	51	No
Arizona	19.8	37	18.6	39	−6.1	28	No
Arkansas	18.6	29	17.1	24	−8.1	20	No
California	23.1	50	22.9	50	−.9	47	No
Colorado	18.7	30	18.0	33	−3.7	40	No
Connecticut	15.0	1	13.3	1	−11.3	10	Yes
Delaware	17.8	22	16.1	18	−9.6	14	No
District of Columbia	18.5	26	13.9	3	−24.9	1	Yes
Florida	19.9	38	17.4	31	−12.6	4	No
Georgia	18.8	31	18.7	40	−.5	48	No
Hawaii	22.7	48	21.6	49	−4.8	33	No
Idaho	20.9	45	20.7	48	−1.0	46	No
Illinois	18.5	26	17.2	27	−7.0	23	No
Indiana	20.0	40	17.9	32	−10.5	11	No
Iowa	16.5	11	15.6	14	−5.5	32	No
Kansas	15.7	5	15.4	12	−1.9	43	No
Kentucky	20.8	44	18.2	35	−12.5	5	No
Louisiana	19.6	35	18.5	38	−5.6	31	No
Maine	18.0	24	14.9	7	−17.2	2	Yes
Maryland	18.5	26	17.1	24	−7.6	21	No
Massachusetts	15.2	3	13.9	3	−8.6	16	Yes
Michigan	22.9	49	20.1	45	−12.2	7	No
Minnesota	17.1	16	17.1	24	.0	49	No
Mississippi	19.3	34	18.8	41	−2.6	42	No
Missouri	17.0	15	16.2	19	−4.7	35	No
Montana	16.5	11	15.8	16	−4.2	38	No
Nebraska	15.7	5	15.1	9	−3.8	39	No
Nevada	21.1	46	20.2	46	−4.3	37	No
New Hampshire	16.8	13	16.0	17	−4.8	33	No
New Jersey	15.9	8	14.0	5	−11.9	9	Yes
New Mexico	18.8	31	18.9	42	.5	50	No
New York	17.6	21	15.2	10	−13.6	3	No
North Carolina	19.9	38	18.2	35	−8.5	18	No
North Dakota	16.8	13	15.6	14	−7.1	22	No
Ohio	19.7	36	18.0	33	−8.6	16	No
Oklahoma	17.2	17	16.9	23	−1.7	45	No
Oregon	20.3	41	18.3	37	−9.9	12	No
Pennsylvania	17.3	19	16.2	19	−6.4	27	No
Rhode Island	16.1	10	15.0	8	−6.8	25	Yes
South Carolina	19.0	33	17.2	27	−9.5	15	No
South Dakota	15.8	7	15.5	13	−1.9	43	No
Tennessee	20.5	42	19.6	44	−4.4	36	No
Texas	18.4	25	17.3	29	−6.0	29	No
Utah	27.4	51	24.7	51	−9.9	12	No
Vermont	15.3	4	13.4	2	−12.4	6	Yes
Virginia	17.8	22	16.3	22	−8.4	19	No
Washington	21.7	47	20.2	46	−6.9	24	No
West Virginia	17.3	19	15.2	10	−12.1	8	No
Wisconsin	17.2	17	16.2	19	−5.8	30	No
Wyoming	15.0	1	14.5	6	−3.3	41	Yes

TABLE 20
State Youth Employment Initiatives

Definition of Adequate State Investment: Does the state allocate funds either to find or create jobs for young people not going on to college?

	School-To-Work Transition Program	Job Creation or Service/ Conservation Corps	Is State's Investment Adequate?
United States Total	Yes 16/No 35	Yes 23/No 28	Yes 28/No 23
Alabama	No	No	No
Alaska	No	Yes	Yes
Arizona	No	Yes	Yes
Arkansas	No	No	No
California	No	Yes	Yes
Colorado	No	Yes	Yes
Connecticut	No	Yes	Yes
Delaware	Yes	No	Yes
District of Columbia	No	No	No
Florida	Yes	Yes	Yes
Georgia	Yes	No	Yes
Hawaii	No	No	No
Idaho	No	No	No
Illinois	No	Yes	Yes
Indiana	No	No	No
Iowa	Yes	Yes	Yes
Kansas	No	No	No
Kentucky	No	No	No
Louisiana	No	No	No
Maine	No	Yes	Yes
Maryland	Yes	Yes	Yes
Massachusetts	Yes	No	Yes
Michigan	Yes	Yes	Yes
Minnesota	No	Yes	Yes
Mississippi	No	No	No
Missouri	No	No	No
Montana	No	Yes	Yes
Nebraska	No	No	No
Nevada	No	No	No
New Hampshire	No	Yes	Yes
New Jersey	Yes	Yes	Yes
New Mexico	No	No	No
New York	Yes	Yes	Yes
North Carolina	Yes	No	Yes
North Dakota	No	No	No
Ohio	Yes	Yes	Yes
Oklahoma	No	No	No
Oregon	Yes	Yes	Yes
Pennsylvania	No	Yes	Yes
Rhode Island	No	No	No
South Carolina	No	No	No
South Dakota	No	No	No
Tennessee	Yes	No	Yes
Texas	No	No	No
Utah	No	No	No
Vermont	Yes	Yes	Yes
Virginia	Yes	Yes	Yes
Washington	No	Yes	Yes
West Virginia	No	No	No
Wisconsin	Yes	Yes	Yes
Wyoming	No	No	No

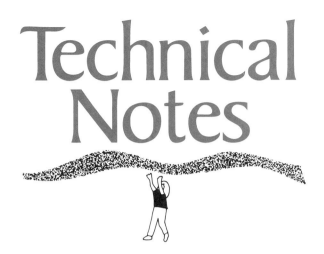

Technical
Notes

International Report Card

Infant Mortality Rate (1988)
    Source of Data: United Nation's Children's Fund (UNICEF), *The State of the World's Children 1990,* Oxford University Press, Oxford, England, 1989.

Mortality Rate for Children Younger than Five (1988)
    Source of Data: UNICEF, *The State of the World's Children 1990.*

Low-Birthweight Births (1988)
    Source of Data: UNICEF, *The State of the World's Children 1990.*

Proportion of One-Year-Olds Fully Immunized Against Polio (latest reported year)
    Source of Data: For all countries except the United States, UNICEF, *The State of the World's Children 1990.* For the United States, data come from the Centers for Disease Control, U.S. Public Health Service, whose latest reported year (1985) is three years behind that of other countries. In 1985 the United States suspended all national childhood immunization statistics collection efforts, and a collection system has not yet been reinstituted.

Number of School-Age Children per Teacher (1986)
    Source of Data: Sivard, Ruth Leger, Brauer, Arlette, and Roemer, Milton, *World Military and Social Expenditures, 13th edition,* World Priorities, Washington, D.C., 1989.

Childhood Poverty Among Eight Industrialized Countries (1979-1982)
    Source of Data: Smeeding, Timothy; Torrey, Barbara Boyle; and Rein, Martin, "Patterns of Income and Poverty: The Economic Status of Children and the Elderly in Eight Countries," *The Vulnerable* (Palmer, Torrey, and Smeeding, ed.), Urban Institute Press, Washington, D.C., 1988.

Mathematical Achievement of Eighth-Grade Students (1981-1982)
Source of Data: U.S. Department of Education, Office of Educational Research and Improvement, *Digest of Educational Statistics, 1988,* CS 88-600, United States Government Printing Office, Washington, D.C., 1989.

Expenditures on Public Education as a Percentage of the Gross National Product Among 14 Selected Nations (1983)
Source of Data: Office of Educational Statistics, *Digest of Educational Statistics.*

Teenage Pregnancy Rates Among Six Selected Nations
Source of Data: Jones, Elise F.; Forest, Jaqueline Darroach; Goldman, Noreen; Henshaw, Stanley; Lincoln, Richard; Rosoff, Jeanie; Westoff, Charles; and Wulf, Diedre, "Teenage Pregnancy in Developed Countries: Determinants and Policy Implications," *Family Planning Perspectives* 17:2 (March/April 1985).

Provision of Medical Care and Financial Assistance to All Pregnant Women
Source of Data: U.S. Department of Health and Human Services, Social Security Administration, Office of Policy, *Social Security Programs Throughout the World 1987,* Research Report #61, United States Government Printing Office, Washington D.C., 1989.

Provision of Medical Care to Workers and their Dependents
Source of Data: U.S. Department of Health and Human Services, *Social Security Programs Throughout the World, 1987.*

Provision of a Family Allowance
Source of Data: U.S. Department of Health and Human Services, *Social Security Programs throughout the World, 1987.*

Provision of Paid Maternity/Parenting Leave Benefits in 17 Industrialized Nations
Source of Data: Kammerman, Sheila, Columbia University, December 1989.

The State Report Card

Table 1: Early Prenatal Care
Source of Data: U.S. Department of Health and Human Services, Public Health Service, National Center for Health Statistics, *Vital Statistics of the United States, 1978, Vol. I—Natality* (1982), Table 1-86; and U.S. Department of Health and Human Services, Public Health Service, National Center for Health Statistics, *Vital Statistics of the United States, 1987, Vol. I—Natality* (1989), Table 1-91.

Early prenatal care is care received during the first three months of pregnancy. In calculating the percentage of births that are to women who received early care, we excluded those births for which the onset of care was unknown.

Table 2: Infant Mortality
Source of Data: U.S. Department of Health and Human Services, Public Health Service, National Center for Health Statistics, *Vital Statistics of the United States,*

1978, Vol. II—Mortality, Part A (1982), Table 2-9; and U.S. Department of Health and Human Services, Public Health Service, National Center for Health Statistics, *Vital Statistics of the United States, 1987, Vol. II— Mortality, Part A* (1989), Table 2-8.

The infant mortality rate is the number of deaths of infants younger than one year old per 1,000 live births in that year.

Table 3: Low-Birthweight Births

Source of Data: U.S. Department of Health and Human Services, Public Health Service, National Center for Health Statistics, *Vital Statistics of the United States, 1978, Vol. I—Natality* (1982), Table 1-77; and U.S. Department of Health and Human Services, Public Health Service, National Center for Health Statistics, *Vital Statistics of the United States, 1987, Vol. I—Natality* (1989), Table 1-82.

Low birthweight is defined as 2,500 grams (5 pounds, 8 ounces) or less. In calculating the percentage of births that are low birthweight, we excluded those births for which the birthweight was unknown.

Table 4: Teen Birth Rates

Source of Data: U.S. Department of Health and Human Services, Public Health Service, National Center for Health Statistics, *Vital Statistics of the United States, 1980, Vol. I—Natality* (1984), Table 1-56; U.S. Department of Health and Human Services, Public Health Service, National Center for Health Statistics, *Vital Statistics of the United States, 1986, Vol. I—Natality* (1988), Table 1-60; U.S. Department of Commerce, Bureau of the Census, *1980 Census of Population*, Volume 1, Characteristics of the Population, Chapter B, General Population Characteristics, Part 1, United States Summary (May 1983), Table 67; and U.S. Department of Commerce, Bureau of the Census, Estimates of the Resident Population of States (unpublished).

The teen birth rate is the number of births to women ages 15 to 19 per 1,000 women of that age.

Table 5: Births to Unmarried Women

Source of Data: U.S. Department of Health and Human Services, Public Health Service, National Center for Health Statistics, *Vital Statistics of the United States, 1980, Vol. I—Natality* (1984), Table 1-36; and U.S. Department of Health and Human Services, Public Health Service, National Center for Health Statistics, *Vital Statistics of the United States, 1987, Vol. I—Natality* (1989), Table 1-36.

The out-of-wedlock birth ratio is the proportion of births that are to unmarried women.

Table 6: Paternities Established

Source of Data: U.S. Department of Health and Human Services, Office of Child Support Enforcement, *Child Support Enforcement Statistics, Fiscal 1981* (June 1982), Table 19; U.S. Department of Health and Human Services, Office of Child Support Enforcement, *Child Support Enforcement: Twelfth Annual Report to Congress for the Period Ending September 30, 1987, Vol. II, Fiscal Year 1987 Statistics* (1988), Table 40; U.S. Department of Health and Human Services, Public Health Service, National Center for Health Statistics, *Vital Statistics of the United States, 1981, Vol. I—Natality* (1985), Table 1-72; and U.S. Department of Health and Human Services, Public Health Service, National Center for Health Statistics, *Vital Statistics of the United States, 1987, Vol. I—Natality* (1989), Table 1-77.

The paternity rate is the number of paternities established per 1,000 births to unmarried women.

Table 7: Children in Poverty

Source of Data: U.S. Department of Commerce, Bureau of the Census, *1980 Census of Population,* Volume 1, Characteristics of the Population, Chapter C, General Social and Economic Characteristics, Part 1, United States Summary (December 1983), Table 245; U.S. Department of Commerce, Bureau of the Census, *Current Population Reports,* Series P-25, No. 1024, State Population and Household Estimates, With Age, Sex, and Components of Change: 1981-87 (May 1988), Table 5; and U.S. Department of Commerce, Bureau of the Census, estimates of the number of poor related children, by state, 1983-1987 (unpublished).

The child poverty rate for 1985 is the average of the calculated child poverty rates for the years 1983-1987. The number of poor children for 1985 is the average of the estimated number of poor children for the years 1983-1987.

Table 8: Affordability of Housing for the Poor

Source of Data: *Federal Register,* Vol. 44, No. 145 (July 26, 1979), pp. 43902-44052; *Federal Register,* Vol. 44, No. 199 (October 12, 1979), pp. 59112-59150; *Federal Register,* Vol. 54, No. 187 (September 28, 1989), pp. 39866-39938; U.S. Department of Commerce, Bureau of the Census, *Current Population Reports,* Series P-60, No. 125, "Money Income and Poverty Status of Families and Persons in the United States: 1979 (Advance Report)," (October 1980), Table 17; U.S. Department of Commerce, Bureau of the Census, *Current Population Reports,* Series P-60, No. 166, "Money Income and Poverty Status in the United States: 1988 (Advance Data) From the March 1989 Current Population Survey" (October 1989), Table A-2; Executive Office of the President, Office of Management and Budget, *Budget of the United States Government, Fiscal Year 1990* (January 1989), p. 3-10; and U.S. Department of Labor, Bureau of Labor Statistics, unpublished Consumer Price Index (CPI-W) (October 1989).

We used the Fair Market Rent as defined and calculated by the U.S. Department of Housing and Urban Development (HUD): the amount equal to or more than what is paid for rent by 45 percent of people or families who have recently moved. HUD calculates this for different apartment sizes and for each metropolitan area. We used the rent for a two-bedroom apartment in the metropolitan area in each state that had the lowest such rent.

We used the 1979 weighted average poverty threshold calculated by the Census Bureau. To obtain the 1989 poverty threshold, we used the 1988 weighted average poverty threshold calculated by the Census Bureau, and adjusted it for actual inflation through September 1989, as calculated by BLS, and for projected inflation for October through December 1989, as calculated by OMB; the total adjustment for inflation was 4.7 percent.

Table 9: High School Graduation

Source of Data: U.S. Department of Education, Office of Planning, Budget and Evaluation, *State Education Performance Chart: Student Performance, Resource*

Inputs, State Reforms, and Population Characteristics, 1982 and 1988 (1989), Columns 15 and 16.

Graduation rates are for public high schools only. The rates are calculated by dividing the number of public high school graduates by the number of public ninth-grade enrollments four years earlier. Ninth-grade enrollments include a prorated portion of the secondary school students who were unclassified by grade. Graduation rates also were corrected for interstate population migration. Information on the number of persons of graduating age receiving GEDs is not available.

Table 10: Youth Unemployment
Source of Data: U.S. Department of Labor, Bureau of Labor Statistics, *Geographic Profile of Employment and Unemployment, 1982* (May 1983), Table 12; and U.S. Department of Labor, Bureau of Labor Statistics, *Geographic Profile of Employment and Unemployment, 1988* (May 1989), Table 12.

The youth unemployment rate is the proportion of persons in the labor force ages 16 to 19 who are unemployed—that is, not employed but looking for work.

Table 11: State Medicaid Coverage of Babies and Pregnant Women
Source of Data: Children's Defense Fund, survey of state Medicaid agencies, October 1989.

Table 12: State Medicaid Coverage of Poor Children
Source of Data: Children's Defense Fund, survey of state Medicaid agencies, October 1989. Technically, children younger than one are termed "infants" in federal Medicaid law. Thus, states that do not cover children older than one are not covering "children" at all. All states will be *required* to provide coverage to all children younger than six in families with incomes less than 133 percent of the federal poverty level by April 1990, according to the recently enacted Budget Reconciliation Act of 1989. States still are allowed to cover poor children up to age eight under federal Medicaid law.

In California, all children younger than 18 living in families with incomes below the poverty level qualify for Medicaid coverage because the state's income thresholds equal or exceed the federal poverty line. In Colorado, Idaho, New Hampshire, and North Dakota, infants (up to age one) qualify for Medicaid if their family income is below 75 or 85 percent of the poverty level; these states, like all others, must increase their eligibility level for poor infants to 133 percent of the poverty level as of April 1990 according to the 1989 Budget Reconciliation Act.

Table 13: Nutritional Assistance to Women and Children
Source of Data: U.S. Department of Agriculture, Food and Nutrition Service, *Estimation of Eligibility for the WIC Program* (July 1987), Table 16; and U.S. Department of Agriculture, Food and Nutrition Service, *WIC Program, State Agency Participation and Expenditure Report* (August 1989, unpublished).

The 1984 WIC eligibility estimates were derived by the Center on Budget and Policy Priorities by multiplying state WIC eligibility figures for 1979 by 25.3 percent, the increase in the number of women, infants, and children nationally who were income-eligible for WIC in 1984 as compared to 1979. WIC participation rates include those served with federal and state funds.

States may supplement federal WIC funds to serve more eligible persons. Ten states appropriate funds to provide food and nutrition. Five states (Indiana, Maine, Michigan, New Hampshire, and Washington) supply funds for nutrition services and program administration costs. Three other states (Arizona, Iowa, and New Jersey) have set aside contingency funds in case the state overspends federal allocations. CDF awarded credit only to those states that provided both food *and* nutrition services to more women and children.

Table 14: State Support for Early Childhood Education

Source of Data: U.S. Department of Health and Human Services, Office of Human Development Services, Administration for Children, Youth and Families, Head Start Bureau, unpublished Head Start Performance Indicator Reports; U.S. Department of Commerce, Bureau of the Census, estimates of the number of poor related children, by state, 1983-1987 (unpublished); and U.S. Department of Health and Human Services, Office of Human Development Services, Administration for Children, Youth and Families, Head Start Bureau, *The Challenge of Coordination: Head Start's Relationship to State Funded Preschool Initiatives, Executive Summary* (May 1988), Table 1.

The number of poor three- to five-year-olds was estimated for each state by calculating the 1985 national proportion of poor children who were ages three to five (19.5 percent) and applying this proportion to the estimated total number of poor children in each state in 1985.

In Ohio, the federal Head Start Bureau study did not report a Head Start supplement by the state, but CDF's Ohio office reported that there was a very small state supplement in 1988.

Table 15: Child Care Quality: Staff Ratios

Source of Data: Gwen Morgan, *The National State of Child Care Regulations, 1989,* Work/Family Directions, Watertown, MA (1989, in press).

The national median is also the number recommended by the National Association for the Education of Young Children (NAEYC) for a high-quality child care program. NAEYC recommends a maximum of three infants per staff member if the group size is limited to six, or four if group size is limited to eight.

Nevada changes from 4:1 to 6:1 at nine months; Tennessee has a ratio of 5:1 or 7:1. In both cases, we chose the more stringent ratio. Hawaii does not allow children younger than two in child care centers.

Table 16: State Child Support Collection Efforts

Source of Data: U.S. Department of Health and Human Services, Office of Child Support Enforcement, *Child Support Enforcement Statistics, Fiscal Year 1988, Vol. II, Thirteenth Annual Report to Congress for the Period Ending September 30, 1988* (December 1988), Tables 37 and 72.

States are supposed to report total child support obligations due for their entire caseload. It is unclear whether all states in fact do this, or whether some report the total obligations only for those cases for which some payment has been made.

Table 17: Change in AFDC Benefits Compared with Inflation

Source of Data: U.S. House of Representatives, Committee on Ways and

Means, *Background Material and Data on Programs Within the Jurisdiction of the Committee on Ways and Means: 1989 Edition* (March 15, 1989), pp. 546-547.

The real percentage change was calculated by the Congressional Research Service using the CPI-U. The January 1989 CPI-U was 361.6; the average CPI-U for 1970 was 116.3.

Table 18: Adequacy of AFDC Benefits in Relation to Housing Costs

Source of Data: *Federal Register,* Vol. 54, No. 187 (September 28, 1989), pp. 39866-39938; and U.S. House of Representatives, Committee on Ways and Means, *Background Material and Data on Programs Within the Jurisdiction of the Committee on Ways and Means: 1989 Edition* (March 15, 1989), pp. 546-547.

We used the Fair Market Rent as defined and calculated by the U.S. Department of Housing and Urban Development (HUD): the amount equal to or more than what is paid for rent by 45 percent of people or families who recently moved. HUD calculates this for different apartment sizes and for each metropolitan area. We have used the rent for a two-bedroom apartment in the metropolitan area in each state that had the lowest such rent, except in Michigan (we used Wayne County) and New York (New York City). We used maximum AFDC benefit levels in each state for a family of three because that is the average size of an AFDC recipient family.

Table 19: Students-per-Teacher Ratios

Source of Data: U.S. Department of Education, Office of Planning, Budget and Evaluation, *State Education Performance Chart: Student Performance, Resource Inputs, State Reforms, and Population Characteristics, 1982 and 1988* (1989), Columns 19 and 20.

The students-per-teacher ratio is the number of public elementary and secondary school students divided by the number of public elementary and secondary full-time-equivalent teachers. "Teachers" includes all teaching staff, not just classroom teachers; librarians, art teachers, and teaching aides are all included in the total. The average *class* size is 24, and the total student–teacher ratio is 18:1, which means that only three-fourths of the "teachers" are classroom teachers. Recommendations by the National Association of Elementary School Principals and the National Education Association for maximum students per classroom teacher of 15 to 1 are based on research suggesting that student achievement is highest with a *class size of 17 to 20,* which translates into a total student–teacher ratio of 15:1 when non-classroom teaching staff is excluded.

Table 20: State Youth Employment Initatives

Source of Data: Children's Defense Fund survey of selected state youth employment agencies, 1989.

Children's Defense Fund
Information Form

☐ Yes! I am going to work hard for children in election year 1990.

I am going to:

☐ Participate in voter registration and get-out-the-vote activities.

☐ Sponsor a candidates' forum on children's issues.

☐ Other (please specify) _____

Please send me the following Children 1990 materials:

Title and Charges	*State*	*Quantity*
State Fact Sheet		
Single-copy, free (please photocopy	_____	1
if you wish to distribute copies)	_____	1
	_____	1

Children 1990 Bumper Stickers
Single-copy, free; 2-50, $3*; 51-100, $7; 101-500, $15 _____

Children 1990 Campaign Posters
Single folded copy, free; 2-50, $4*; 51-100, $10; 101-500, $20 _____

Flat version, on durable stock, $4.95 per poster _____

An Advocate's Guide to the Media
$4.95 per copy _____

☐ I would like to support CDF's Children 1990 Campaign. Enclosed is my check for

$ _____. (Contributions are tax deductible to the full extent of the law.)

*Postage and handling charges only. For larger bulk orders, contact CDF's Children 1990 desk at (202) 628-8787.

NAME _____

TITLE _____

ADDRESS _____

CITY, STATE, ZIP _____

DAYTIME TELEPHONE NUMBER (_____) _____

ZIP CODE OF HOME ADDRESS _____

Please detach this form and mail in an envelope to: Children 1990, Children's Defense Fund, 122 C Street N.W., Washington, D.C. 20001. Include check, payable to Children's Defense Fund, to cover any charges. Sorry, orders without payment cannot be processed because of the large volume of responses we receive.

What is CDF?

The Children's Defense Fund (CDF) exists to provide a strong and effective voice for the children of America who cannot vote, lobby, or speak out for themselves. We pay particular attention to the needs of poor, minority, and disabled children. Our goal is to educate the nation about the needs of children and encourage preventive investment in children before they get sick, drop out of school, suffer family breakdown, or get into trouble.

CDF is a unique organization. CDF focuses on programs and policies that affect large numbers of children, rather than on helping families on a case-by-case basis. Our staff includes specialists in health, education, child welfare, mental health, child development, adolescent pregnancy prevention, and youth employment. CDF gathers data and disseminates information on key issues affecting children. We monitor the development and implementation of federal and state policies. We provide information, technical assistance, and support to a network of state and local child advocates. We pursue an annual legislative agenda in the U.S. Congress and litigate selected cases of major importance. CDF's major initiatives include our adolescent pregnancy prevention program and a prenatal and child health campaign. CDF educates thousands of citizens annually about children's needs and responsible policy options for meeting those needs. CDF is a national organization with roots in communities across America. Although our main office is in Washington, D.C., we reach out to towns and cities across the country to monitor the effects of changes in national and state policies and to help people and organizations concerned with what happens to children. CDF maintains state offices in Minnesota, Ohio, and Texas. CDF has developed cooperative projects with groups in many states.

CDF is a private nonprofit organization supported by foundations, corporate grants, and individual donations.